STUDY NOTES

CURRENT AFFAIRS MARCH 2023

CONTENT TABLE

CURRENT AFFAIRS MARCH 2023

MARCH 2023 CURRENT AFFAIRS

Important Days News

World Seagrass Day 2023 observed on 1st March

- World Seagrass Day is celebrated annually on 1st March to raise awareness about seagrass and its important functions in the marine ecosystem.
- The seagrasses are grass-like plants that live close to the sea. They are the only flowering plant to grow in the marine environment. There are more than 60 seagrass species in the world. They act as the best carbon sink and provide food for marine life.
- The seagrasses have been declining since the 1930s. International Union for Conservation of Nature (IUCN) categorizes nearly 21% of the world's seagrasses as near threatened or vulnerable or endangered. Pollution, coastal development activities, and land-based run-offs are degrading the seagrasses.

World Civil Defence Day 2023 celebrated on 01st March

- World Civil Defence Day is observed on 1st March to raise awareness about the importance of civil defence measures in protecting people and their property from natural disasters, accidents, and other emergencies.
- The day honours the work of several civil defence organisations. The day also recognises the efforts put in by the organisations in protecting communities and saving lives. The day also recognises the contribution of civil defence personnel, who work tirelessly to ensure the safety and well-being of their communities.
- The theme for this year is "Uniting the world's leading specialists for the safety and security of future generations.

World Wildlife Day 2023 celebrates on 3rd March

- Every 3rd of March, wildlife is celebrated all over the world for the UN World Wildlife Day. This date was chosen as it is the birthday of CITES, the Convention on International Trade in Endangered Species of Wild Fauna and Flora, signed in 1973.
- This global event is marked annually to celebrate and promote awareness of the planet's wild fauna and flora.
- The date also marks the adoption of the Convention on International Trade in Endangered Species of Wild Fauna and Flora (CITES) in 1973. CITES aims to prevent international trade from threatening species' survival.

National Security Day 2023 observed on 04th March

- India celebrates National Security Day on March 4 every year. Rashtriya Suraksha Diwas is another name for it, and it is a holiday honouring the Indian Security Forces.
- The purpose of the National Security Day is to express gratitude to our nation's security forces, which include the police, paramilitary units, guards, commandos, army officers, and other units involved in preserving the safety and security of our citizens.
- The National Safety Council of India announced the theme for this year to be 'Nurture young minds – Develop safety culture'. The NSC announces a new theme for the year to celebrate the week-long celebration.

International News

Australia's Deakin University to set up campus in GIFT city

- The first foreign university to establish a campus in India will be Deakin University of Australia. The autonomous campus will be built in Gujarat International Financial Tec-City (GIFT) City.
- While visiting Ahmedabad, Australian Prime Minister Anthony Norman Albanese is anticipated to make the official announcement.
- According to the QS World University Rankings, Deakin University is ranked 266 overall. It is one of the top 50 new universities worldwide.
- At least two Australian institutions are considering opening campuses in India.

International Yoga Festival 2023 Held on Banks of Ganges in Rishikesh

- The International Yoga Festival 2023 will be held in Rishikesh from 1st March to 7th March 2023. The International Yoga Festival 2023 is the main attraction of Bharat Parv this year.

- The six-day event of the International Yoga Festival 2023 will promote the rich heritage and diverse natural wonders of the state and it is a significant point of discussion among those visiting the Uttarakhand Tourism pavilion at the event held in Red Fort.

Uranium particles enriched up to 83.7 per cent found in Iran: UN report

- Inspectors from the United Nations nuclear watchdog found uranium particles enriched up to 83.7% in Iran's underground Fordo nuclear site.
- The confidential quarterly report by the Vienna-based International Atomic Energy Agency distributed to member states likely will raise tensions further between Iran and the West over its nuclear program.
- That's even as Tehran already faces internal unrest after months of protests and Western anger over sending bomb-carrying drones to Russia for its war on Ukraine.
- The IAEA report only speaks about "particles," suggesting that Iran isn't building a stockpile of uranium enriched above 60% — the level it has been enriching at for some time.

Ales Bialiatski, Nobel laureate sentenced prison for 10 years in Belarus

- Ales Bialiatski, a leading defender of human rights in Belarus and a candidate for the 2022 Nobel Peace Prize, was given a 10-year prison term in Minsk, the Capital of Belarus.
- Ales Bialiatski and three other key members of the Viasna human rights organisation he created were found guilty of funding rallies against the government.

5th ASEAN-India Business Summit 2023

- The 5th Asean-India Business Summit took place on 6 March 2023 in Kuala Lumpur.
- Speakers and participants from Asean and India convened to discuss how business linkages, connectivity and supply chain resilience can be enhanced through deeper ASEAN-India cooperation.
- The Minister of State for Electronics & Information Technology addresses the 5th ASEAN-India Business summit.

Xi Jinping starts third term as China's president

- Xi Jinping began an unprecedented third term as China's president after he was endorsed by a unanimous vote from the 2,977-member National People's Congress (NPC).
- Xi will head a hand-picked party and government team tasked with steering the world's second-largest economy through challenges at home and abroad over the next five years.

India & Sri Lanka inaugurate exhibition 'Geoffrey Bawa' in New Delhi

- India's External Affairs Minister, S Jaishankar, inaugurated the "Geoffrey Bawa:
- It is Essential To Be There" exhibition at the National Gallery of Modern Art in New Delhi.
- The exhibition, which is a joint collaboration between the National Gallery of Modern Art in New Delhi, the High Commission of Sri Lanka in New Delhi, and the Geoffrey Bawa Trust, showcases the architectural works of Sri Lanka's renowned architect, the late Geoffrey Bawa.

Japan, U.S., South Korea, Taiwan launch 'Chip 4' talks for supply chain

- Japan, the United States, South Korea and Taiwan have held the first meeting of senior officials under a new U.S.-led framework to help ensure a stable supply of semiconductors, Japan's industry ministry said.
- Officials from industry organizations in the four economies took part in the virtual conference of the "Chip 4" alliance on Feb. 16 to discuss ways to maintain supply chain resilience in times of natural disasters and other contingencies.
- In a bid to outcompete China technologically, the Biden administration launched a new dialogue forum with Japan and South Korea on friend-shoring semiconductors as it invites companies to compete for a share of the $50 billion already approved to revitalize the U.S. chip industry.
- The inaugural meeting of the Economic Security Dialogue among the United States, Japan and South Korea was launched in Honolulu.
- Japan and South Korea are home to two of the world's strongest semiconductor industries, and the forum aims to address issues related to critical and emerging technologies, supply chain resilience of semiconductors, batteries and critical minerals, as well as data transparency amid the U.S.-China tech war.

PFRDA raises ombudsman age limit to 70 years from 65 years

- The government increased the maximum age for Pension Fund Regulatory and Development Authority's (PFRDA) ombudsman from 65 to 70 years.
- The ombudsman is responsible for receiving, evaluating, and helping to resolve complaints or grievances that come under PFRDA regulations.

The Windsor framework: The deal between UK and EU

- After months of intensive talks, the United Kingdom and European Union have unveiled an agreement on the Northern Ireland Protocol, called the Windsor Framework.
- This is not a new protocol or a fundamental rewrite of the current treaty. But the package announced this week is an improved deal that could substantively ease how the protocol will operate for businesses as well as individuals.
- It is a negotiating achievement that marks a turning point in the long road since Brexit for Northern Ireland.

What is POTS, a disease which affected 1 million Americans after Covid

- POTS or postural orthostatic tachycardia syndrome has affected around three million Americans before Covid-19 and at least one million new patients after the pandemic. Many people are still not familiar with the disease. A study reveals that around 2% to 14% of people with covid develop POTS.
- The majority of people with POTS are women and people assigned female at birth aged 15 to 50 years. But men and people assigned male at birth can also have POTS.

Vietnam parliament elects Vo Van Thuong as new president

- The country is changing its top leadership as it continues its anti-corruption campaign. The National Assembly(NA) of the Socialist Republic of Vietnam elected Vo Van Thuong(Võ Văn Thưởng) (52 years old), a member of the Politburo of the Communist Party of Vietnam, as the new President of Vietnam for a term running until 2026.
- Mr. Vo Van Thuong took oath as the new president of Vietnam during the National Assembly's extraordinary meeting in Hanoi, Vietnam. Vương Đình Huệ, Chairman of NA, on behalf of the parliament has recognised the oath of the new President.

Why is Indonesia moving its capital from Jakarta to Borneo?

- Indonesia is all set to move its capital from Jakarta to Borneo over environmental issues such as being congested, sinking into seawater, and being prone to earthquakes.

- Officials said the new metropolis city will be a "sustainable forest city," that puts the environment at the heart of the development and will be carbon neutral by 2045.
- Indonesian President Joko Widodo envisions the construction of the new capital as a "nostrum for the problems in Jakarta, which will also allow the country to start afresh."

Colombia opens military service to women for first time in 25 years

- Colombia has opened military service to women for the first time in 25 years. A cohort of 1,296 women have been enlisted in Colombia's Army in the month of February.
- Recruits must live on military bases for several months and earn a monthly stipend of only about $75, but some of the women in the new program hope it helps them build a career in the armed forces. They see it as a chance for a stable job and educational opportunities.
- Colombia has long had compulsory military service for men ages 18 to 24. The army relies heavily on those young recruits to staff bases, protect infrastructure and carry out administrative tasks, while its professional soldiers confront drug trafficking gangs and rebel groups.

Indonesia's Mount Merapi volcano erupts, covering villages in ash

- Mount Merapi, one of the world's most active volcanoes, erupted, spewing out smoke and ash that covered villages near the crater.
- There were no immediate reports of casualties, the the National Disaster Mitigation Agency said.
- The images broadcasted shows ash-covered houses and roads at a village near the volcano, in Yogyakarta.

Denmark, the first country to import CO2 and bury it undersea

- Denmark inaugurates a project to store carbon dioxide 1,800 metres beneath the North Sea, the first country in the world to bury CO2 imported from abroad.
- The CO2 graveyard, where the carbon is injected to prevent further warming of the atmosphere, is on the site of an old oil field.

- Led by British chemical giant Ineos and German oil company Wintershall Dea, the "Greensand" project is expected to store up to eight million tonnes of CO2 per year by 2030.

Bhutan's graduation from the UN list of Least Developed Countries

- Recently, at the United Nations Least Developed Countries (LDC) Summit that concluded on March 9 in Doha, Qatar, the landlocked Himalayan kingdom of Bhutan will no longer be on the list of LDCs and will become only the seventh country to graduate from the list.
- Bhutan was included in the first group of LDCs in 1971. However, over the last few decades, it has made remarkable progress on a variety of socio-economic metrics.
- Bhutan first fulfilled the requirements for graduation in 2015, and then again in 2018. Bhutan was therefore scheduled to graduate in 2021.
- However, the UN viewed Bhutan's request to match the effective graduation date with the conclusion of the nation's 12th national development plan in 2023 as a legitimate request and thus postponed the delisting.

India-Bangladesh Friendship Pipeline to be jointly inaugurated by PM Modi and Sheikh Hasina

- Prime Minister Narendra Modi, and his Bangladesh counterpart Sheikh Hasina, will inaugurate the India-Bangladesh Friendship Pipeline via video conference.
- It is first such pipeline through which refined diesel will be supplied to Bangladesh from India.
- The project is built under grant assistance from the government of India.
- The project involves construction of 130-kilometre long pipeline that will connect Siliguri in West Bengal and Parbatipur in Dinajpur district of Bangladesh.
- Of the total stretch, six-kilometre will be in Indian side and remaining 124 kilometres will in Bangladesh. Indian leg of the pipeline project will be implemented by Assam-based Numaligarh Refinery Limited and Bangladeshi leg will be implemented by Bangladesh Petroleum Corporation.

ICC issues arrest warrant for Vladimir Putin over Ukraine war crimes

- The International Criminal Court (ICC) issued an arrest warrant for Russian President Vladimir Putin over the forced transfer of children to Russia after the Kremlin's invasion of Ukraine.

- Ukrainians accuse Russia of attempting genocide against them and seeking to destroy their identity — partly through deporting children to Russia.
- The ICC issued the warrant for Putin's arrest on suspicion of unlawful deportation of children and unlawful transfer of people from the territory of Ukraine to the Russian Federation.

US recognized McMahon Line as international border

- A bipartisan resolution was passed by the US, formally recognizing the McMahon Line as the international boundary between China and India's Arunachal Pradesh.
- The resolution rejected China's claim that the state belongs to its territory and instead acknowledged Arunachal Pradesh as an integral part of India.
- Furthermore, the resolution expressed support for India's sovereignty and territorial integrity.

Bangladesh commissions its first submarine base

- Prime Minister Sheikh Hasina inaugurated the first submarine base of Bangladesh 'BNS Sheikh Hasina' at Pekua in Cox's Bazar.
- Hailing the newly inaugurated naval base as an 'ultra modern submarine base', Prime Minister called the event a proud chapter in the history of Bangladesh navy.
- This is the first ever full-fledged submarine base of Bangladesh Navy.
- Built at a cost of $1.21 billion.
- The base can accommodatc a total of six submarines and eight warships at a time.

Japanese PM Kishida invites PM Modi to G7 Hiroshima summit

- Japanese Prime Minister Fumio Kishida has formally invited Prime Minister Narendra Modi to the G7 Summit after both had a delegation-level talk at Delhi's Hyderabad House.
- PM Modi said that PM Kishida's visit will be helpful to maintain a momentum of mutual cooperation between India and Japan.
- He pointed out the importance of leading two significant summits, G20 and G7, by respective countries.

Egypt joins BRICS bank as new member weeks after President Sisi's India visit

- After President Abdel-Fattah El-Sisi visited India as a chief guest for the Republic Day celebrations, Egypt has become a member of the BRICS New Development Bank (NDB).
- According to sources familiar with the matter, Egypt officially joined the NDB on February 20, with a formal notification issued on March 22.
- The African-Arab nation intends to enhance its infrastructure, and NDB funding can make a significant contribution toward achieving this goal.

Jack Dorsey's wealth tumbles $526 million after Hindenburg short

- Hindenburg Research's recent report accusing Block Inc. of ignoring extensive fraud has had a significant impact on co-founder Jack Dorsey's net worth.
- His fortune experienced its most substantial single-day decline since May, with a drop of 11%, resulting in a decrease of $526 million.
- According to the Bloomberg Billionaires Index, Dorsey's net worth now stands at $4.4 billion.

China spent $240 billion bailing out 'Belt & Road' countries: Study

- A recent study conducted by researchers from the World Bank, Harvard Kennedy School, AidData, and the Kiel Institute for the World Economy has revealed that China spent approximately $240 billion from 2008 to 2021 bailing out 22 developing countries that had difficulty repaying loans taken for Belt and Road infrastructure projects.
- A recently published study shows that from 2008 to 2021, China provided approximately $240 billion to bail out 22 developing nations that encountered challenges in paying back loans obtained for the Belt and Road infrastructure projects.

Former Brazilian President Dilma Rousseff named new President of BRICS New Development Bank

- The New Development Bank (NDB), which is also known as the BRICS bank and is a multilateral financial institution created by Brazil, Russia, India, China, and South Africa, has announced that former Brazilian President Dilma Vana Rousseff has been elected as its new President.

- She replaces Marcus Troyjo in the position. Dilma Rousseff is an economist who served as the President of the Federative Republic of Brazil for two consecutive terms, from January 2011 to August 2016.

Saudi Arabia becomes Shanghai Cooperation Organization dialogue partner

- The Saudi Arabian government has taken a significant step towards joining the Shanghai Cooperation Organization (SCO), a regional alliance dominated by China and Russia.
- During a cabinet meeting presided over by King Salman bin Abdulaziz, a memorandum was approved to initiate dialogue with the SCO.
- The decision to pursue membership was reportedly raised during a visit to Saudi Arabia by Chinese President Xi Jinping in December of last year.

Tanzania announces outbreak of deadly Marburg virus disease

- The northwestern Kagera region of Tanzania has been declared an epidemic zone by the country's leaders after five people died and three others were diagnosed with Marburg viral disease (MVD) at a local hospital.
- The World Health Organization (WHO) has identified 161 individuals who are at risk of contracting the virus through contact tracing.

Economy News

India's manufacturing PMI slips to 4-month low of 55.3 in February

- India's purchasing managers' index (PMI) declined to a 4-month low at 55.3 in February owing to a rise in input costs, according to the S&P Global India Manufacturing PMI report.
- In January, the manufacturing PMI stood at 55.4. The headline figure, however, remained above its long-run average of 53.7. A reading above 50 indicates an overall increase in output compared to the previous month.
- Input costs in the manufacturing industry increased further, with firms mentioning higher prices for electronic components, energy, foodstuff, metals and textiles, says the report.
- Despite quickening to a four-month high, the rate of inflation was below its long-run average and among the weakest in over two years

Moody's expects India to report real GDP growth of 5.5 percent in 2023

- Moody's now expects India's real GDP growth to be 5.5% in 2023, up from the earlier projection of 5%, and to be 6.5% in 2024.
- The upward revisions for India also incorporate a significant increase in capital expenditure budget allocation to ₹10 lakh crore (3.3% of GDP) for fiscal year 2023-24, up from ₹7.5 lakh crore for the fiscal year ending in March 2023.
- Moody's has published its macro-outlook for G20 economies and has made upward revisions to its 2023 growth forecasts for the US, the euro area and China. Additionally, the credit rating agency has raised growth projections for India, Mexico, Russia, Saudi Arabia and Türkiye.

India's UPI likely to extend to UAE, Mauritius, Indonesia

- India's Unified Payments Interface (UPI) is shortly to be connected to comparable networks in Indonesia, Mauritius, and the United Arab Emirates (UAE). This occurs a week after Singapore's PayNow launched cross-border connection for real-time digital payments.
- The Indian diaspora will soon be able to quickly and cheaply deal across international borders by scanning QR codes.
- To facilitate quicker remittances between the two nations, Singapore's PayNow network and India's UPI were connected.

India's GDP growth slows to 4.4% in October-December quarter

- India's gross domestic product (GDP) growth rate fell for the second straight quarter in the October-December period, coming in at 4.4 percent, the Ministry of Statistics and Programmed Implementation said.
- At 4.4 percent, the latest quarterly growth number is lower than the 6.3 percent growth that was recorded in the second quarter of 2022-23, which itself was less than half the 13.2 percent increase posted in April-June 2022 as the GDP growth rate benefitted from a low base in the early part of the year.

India's Unemployment rate rose to 7.45% in Feb: CMIE

- Joblessness as measured by the CMIE All India unemployment rate remained elevated in February 2023 and rose to 7.45% from 7.14% in the previous month.
- The urban unemployment rate decreased for the second straight month and was at 7.93% in February as against 8.55% in January.

- It touched a record high of 10.09% in December 2022. But more worrying the rural unemployment rate spiked to 7.23% last month from 6.48% in January.

India's per capita income doubles since 2014-15: NSO

- India's per capita income in nominal terms doubled to Rs 1,72,000 since 2014-15 when the Narendra Modi-led NDA came to power but uneven income distribution remains a challenge.
- As per the National Statistical Office (NSO), the annual per capita (net national income) at current prices is estimated at Rs 1,72,000 in 2022-23, up from Rs 86,647 in 2014-15, suggesting an increase of about 99 per cent.
- In real terms (constant prices), the per capita income has increased by about 35 per cent from Rs 72,805 in 2014-15 to Rs 98,118 in 2022-23.

India's WPI inflation eases to 3.85 per cent in February

- India's Wholesale price index (WPI)-based inflation eased below the 4 per cent-mark in February and was recorded at 3.85 per cent, data released by the Ministry of Commerce and Industry showed. In January, the WPI inflation figure was 4.73 per cent.
- This is the lowest since January 2021 when the WPI inflation was 2.51 per cent.
- According to the data released, the decline in the rate of inflation in February is primarily due to the fall in prices of crude petroleum & natural gas, non-food articles, food products, minerals, computer, electronic & optical products, chemicals & chemical products, electrical equipment and motor vehicles, trailers & semi-trailers.

India's retail inflation drops to 6.44% in February 2023

- India's retail inflation for February slows down to 6.44 percent as against 6.52 percent in January 2023, according to data published by the Ministry of Statistics and Programme Implementation on March 13.
- While the CPI in January stood at 6.52 percent, the same for December 2022 was at 5.72 percent. In November, it was 5.88 percent and 5.59 percent in October 2022.
- Rise in food prices, which account for nearly half of the CPI basket, moderated last month to 5.95% from 6% in January. However, the bulk of the slowdown probably came from easing international prices and the government's efforts to provide additional supplies of wheat.

CRISIL forecasts India's GDP growth at 6% for next FY against NSO's projection of 7%

- CRISIL expects India's gross domestic product (GDP) growth to touch 6% in fiscal 2024, compared with 7% estimated by the National Statistics Office (NSO) for fiscal 2023.
- A complex interplay of geopolitical events, stubbornly high inflation — and sharp rate hikes to counter that — have turned the global environment gloomier.
- On the domestic front, the peak impact of the rate hikes — 250 basis points since May 2022, which has pushed interest rates above pre-Covid-19 levels — will play out in fiscal 2024.

OECD raises FY24 India growth forecast to 5.9 per cent

- The Organisation for Economic Cooperation and Development (OECD) has in creased its growth projection for India by 20 basis points to 5.9% for the fiscal year 2024, according to its latest interim outlook report titled "Fragile Recovery."
- The report also predicts that India's GDP will grow by 6.9% in the fiscal year 2023, and around 7% in the following fiscal year, despite tighter financial conditions.
- The report also highlighted some positive signs of improvement in the global economy, but warned that the outlook remains fragile due to risks such as the war in Ukraine, monetary policy changes, and pressures in global energy markets.

Income tax dept launches mobile app AIS for Taxpayers

- On March 22, the Income Tax Department launched a mobile application called "AIS for Taxpayer" that enables taxpayers to view their tax-related information in the Annual Information Statement (AIS) or Taxpayer Information Summary (TIS).
- The app has become essential and beneficial since starting from the new financial year on April 1, Form 26AS will only show information related to tax de ducted at source (TDS) and tax collection at source (TCS).
- Taxpayers need to refer to the AIS for various details, including installments of advance tax paid, self-assessment tax, income-tax refund, Statement of Financial Transactions (SFT), and turnover as per Goods and Service Tax (GST) return, among other things.

Cabinet hikes Dearness Allowance (DA) by 4% for central government employees, pensioners

- The Union Cabinet approved an increase in the dearness allowance and dearness relief by 4 per cent to 42 per cent, benefiting 47.58 lakh central government employees and 69.76 lakh pensioners.
- According to I&B Minister Anurag Thakur, the combined impact of both the Dearness Allowance and Dearness Relief on the exchequer will be Rs 12,815.60 crore annually.

Finance Bill 2023 passed in Lok Sabha

- The Lok Sabha passed the Finance Bill 2023, which implements tax proposals for the upcoming fiscal year, without any discussion.
- The passage of the Bill occurred amid Opposition uproar over the Adani controversy.
- Proposals for a total of 64 official amendments were put forward in the Bill, including one that aims to eliminate long-term tax benefits for specific categories of debt mutual funds and another that calls for the establishment of the GST Appellate Tribunal.

EPFO hikes interest rate on employees' provident fund to 8.15% for 2022-23

- The Employees' Provident Fund Organisation (EPFO) has increased the interest rate on employees' provident fund (EPF) deposits for the financial year 2022-23.
- At its meeting, the retirement fund body has fixed the interest rate at 8.15 per cent.
- However, this rate is subject to approval by the Ministry of Finance, which ratifies the interest rate provided by the EPFO.
- The interest rate for EPF deposits for the previous year was 8.10 per cent, which was the lowest in over 40 years.
- In addition to discussing the interest rate on EPF deposits for the financial year 2022-23, the CBT will also review the annual accounts of the EPFO.
- The trustees will also deliberate on the implementation of the Supreme Court order, which grants Employees' Pension Scheme 1995 subscribers a four-month window to opt for a higher pension.
- The EPFO has provided its subscribers with the option to select a higher pension until May 3, 2023.

S&P keeps India's economic growth forecast unchanged at 6% for FY24

- S&P Global Ratings has maintained its earlier projection for India's economic growth rate at 6% in the fiscal year starting from April 1, with a further increase to 6.9% in the following year.
- In its latest quarterly economic update for Asia-Pacific, S&P predicted that the inflation rate would decline to 5% during the 2023-24 fiscal year, down from the current financial year's 6.8%.
- The report stated that India's gross domestic product (GDP) is likely to grow by 7% in the present financial year, which ends on March 31, 2023, before slowing down to 6% in the subsequent fiscal year 2023-24.

India's overall exports cross all time high of 750 Billion US dollars

- During the ASSOCHAM Annual Session 2023, Mr. Piyush Goyal, who serves as the Union Minister of Commerce and Industry, Consumer Affairs, Food and Public Distribution, and Textiles, declared that India's merchandise and services exports are expected to surpass US$ 760 billion in the present fiscal year, which will end on March 31, 2023.
- Despite the global economic downturn, rising inflation, and high-interest rates, Mr. Goyal highlighted India's successful performance.
- He also stated that exports increased from US$ 500 billion in 2020-21 to US$ 676 billion in 2021–22.

Cabinet hikes Dearness Allowance (DA) by 4% for central government employees, pensioners

- The Union Cabinet approved an increase in the dearness allowance and dearness relief by 4 per cent to 42 per cent, benefiting 47.58 lakh central government employees and 69.76 lakh pensioners.
- According to I&B Minister Anurag Thakur, the combined impact of both the Dearness Allowance and Dearness Relief on the exchequer will be Rs 12,815.60 crore annually.

Appointments News

Rajesh Malhotra named principal director general of PIB

- Senior Indian Information Service (IIS) officer, Rajesh Malhotra has been appointed as the principal director general of the Press Information Bureau (PIB), according to the Ministry of Information & Broadcasting. He will be the principal spokesperson of the government of India. He will replace Satyendra Prakash, who took charge as principal DG of PIB in August 2022.
- Malhotra, a 1989 batch officer, had been working in Ministry of Finance since January 2018. "During the critical Covid-19 pandemic, he effectively steered the media and communication policy in the Ministry of Finance in sync with the various AatmaNirbhar Bharat Packages announced by the government over time to give relief to people and maintain economic balance,"

Nepal elects Ram Chandra Paudel as its next president

- Ram Chandra Paudel has been elected to serve as the new president of Nepal.
- According to the Nepalese Election Commission, he received 33,800 electoral votes, while his opponent, Subash Chandra Nembwang, received 15,500 votes.
- Ram Chandra Paudel received votes from 352 members of provincial assemblies and 214 members of parliament.

Women's World Boxing Championships 2023: MC Mary Kom, Farhan Akhtar named brand ambassadors

- The Indira Gandhi Sports Complex in New Delhi will host the IBA Women's World Boxing Championship 2023 from March 15–26.
- Mahindra has been named the title sponsor of this competition by the Boxing Federation of India (BFI), while MC Mary Kom and Bollywood actor Farhan Akhtar have been named as brand ambassadors.
- The third time in history, India is serving as the host country. The BFI's goal of promoting female boxing involvement will be greatly enhanced by the appearance of Marykom and Bollywood superstar Farhan Akhtar.

UAE President appoints Sheikh Mansour as Vice-President

- The UAE President, Sheikh Mohamed bin Zayed Al Nahyan, has appointed his brother, Sheikh Mansour bin Zayed Al Nahyan, as the Vice President of the country.
- The appointment was endorsed by the UAE Federal Supreme Council. Sheikh Mohammed bin Rashid Al Maktoum, the current Vice President, will continue to hold the same position.

- Additionally, Sheikh Mohamed, who is also the Ruler of Abu Dhabi, has designated Sheikh Tahnoun bin Zayed and Sheikh Hazza bin Zayed as the Deputy Rulers of Abu Dhabi.

Indian Industrialist Shri Ratan Tata appointed in 'Order of Australia' for distinguished service

- Ratan Tata, an Indian industrialist and philanthropist, has been named an Honorary Officer in the General Division of the Order of Australia (AO) for his outstanding contributions to the Australia-India bilateral relationship, specifically in the areas of trade, investment, and philanthropy.

- The announcement was made by Australia's Governor-General, following a recommendation by Australia's High Commissioner to India, Barry O'Farrell.

- Ratan Tata, who is the Chairman Emeritus of Tata Sons and a former Chairman of the Tata Group, is recognized as one of the wealthiest entrepreneurs worldwide, with a net worth exceeding $1 billion as of 2022.

Eric Garcetti appointed as US Ambassador to India

- The US Senate Committee has announced the appointment of Eric Garcetti as the new US Ambassador to India.
- Despite being nominated by President Joe Biden almost two years ago, Garcetti's appointment had been pending until now.
- Eric Garcetti served as the President of the City Council of Los Angeles for four consecutive terms and is known to be a close acquaintance of President Biden. He has also emerged as a leader within the Democratic Party.
- However, Garcetti's tenure as mayor of Los Angeles lasted for nine years and was not without controversy. In 2020, there was a controversial incident that occurred during his time in office.

FIFA president Gianni Infantino re-elected for another term

- Gianni Infantino was re-elected as FIFA president until 2027 by acclamation, after highlighting his strong financial performance as a reason for keeping a CEO in their position for life.

- The decision was made by the congress of 211 member federations, who have seen their annual funding from FIFA increase from $250,000 to $2 million since Infantino's first win in 2016.
- Following the 2022 World Cup in Qatar, FIFA now has $4 billion in reserves, and it conservatively predicts a record revenue of at least $11 billion from the 2026 men's World Cup, which will be hosted in North America.

Humza Yousaf elected leader of Scottish National party

- Humza Yousaf, a Pakistani-origin politician, has won the Scottish National Party (SNP) leadership contest and is set to become Scotland's First Minister, replacing Nicola Sturgeon.
- Yousaf, who is the son of Asian immigrants, is poised to become the first person of colour to serve as Scotland's first minister.
- He defeated Kate Forbes, the country's finance minister, and Ash Regan, who resigned from the government in opposition to proposed changes to gender recognition.
- Humza Yousaf won the Scottish National Party leadership contest with 52% of the final votes, and his campaign focused on achieving Scottish independence and addressing the cost-of-living crisis.
- This follows Rishi Sunak's recent appointment as the first British Prime Minister of Indian origin.
- Yousaf will now take over as the leader of the SNP, succeeding Nicola Sturgeon who resigned last month after serving as the party leader for eight years.

Ram Sahaya Prasad Yadav becomes Nepal's third Vice President

- Ram Sahaya Prasad Yadav, a leader of the Janata Samajbadi Party, has won the election to become Nepal's third Vice President.
- He was able to secure victory over Astalaxmi Shakya of CPN (UML) and Ma mata Jha of the Janamat Party with support from Nepali Congress, CPN (Maoist Centre), and the CPN (Unified Socialist) including the ruling alliance.
- The election was held today with participation from 311 federal lawmakers and 518 Provincial Assembly members.
- The polling centre for the election was located at the New Baneshwor-based Federal Parliament Building in Kathmandu.

Jishnu Barua appoints as new chairperson of Central Electricity Regulatory Commission

- Jishnu Barua has become the new chairperson of power regulator Central Electricity Regulatory Commission (CERC).
- Barua has been appointed chairperson of the CERC on February 27, 2023.
- Barua was chief secretary of Assam from October 2020 to August 2022. Prior to this, he had been additional chief secretary to Assam looking after various departments of the state from August 2017 to October 2020.

Group Captain Shaliza Dhami 1st woman to command frontline IAF combat unit

- In the first command appointment for a woman officer in the Indian Air Force (IAF), Group Captain Shaliza Dhami has been selected to take over the command of a frontline combat unit in the Western sector.
- For the first time ever in the IAF's history, a woman officer has been given command of a frontline combat unit – in this case, a missile squadron in the Western sector.
- The IAF's move comes just two months after Captain Shiva Chauhan of the Indian Army's Fire and Fury Corps became the first woman officer to be operationally deployed at the world's highest battlefield in Siachen.

Savlon India appoints Sachin Tendulkar as world's first 'Hand Ambassador'

- Savlon revealed the God of Cricket, Sachin Tendulkar as its world's first 'Hand Ambassador' for its Swasth India Mission.
- The campaign features a series of films featuring Sachin Tendulkar's Hand as their chief protagonist – bringing the importance of hand hygiene to everyone's notice.

Amir Tamim appoints Sheikh Mohammed as Qatar's new prime minister

- Qatar's Amir Sheikh Tamim bin Hamad Al Thani has appointed Foreign Minister Sheikh Mohammed bin Abdulrahman Al-Thani as the country's new prime minister.
- The decision to appoint Sheikh Mohammed, who was the deputy prime minister, came after the amir accepted the resignation of former Prime Minister Sheikh Khalid bin Khalifa bin Abdulaziz Al Thani.

- Sheikh Khalid was appointed as Qatar's prime minister and minister of interior in January 2020.

Arun Subramanian becomes 1st Indian-American judge at New York Court

- Arun Subramanian, an attorney, has been appointed as the first Indian American judge of the Manhattan Federal District Court in New York.
- The nomination of Mr. Subramanian for the United States District Court for the Southern District of New York was first made public by US President Joe Biden in September 2022. The Senate confirmed the nomination of Subramanian by a vote of 58-37.

Honeywell appoints veteran Vimal Kapur as CEO

- Honeywell International HON announced that company current president and chief operating officer, Vimal Kapur, will succeed Darius Adamczyk as the new chief executive officer (CEO), effective Jun 1.
- He has also been named to the board of directors of HON as of March 13. He has 34 years of experience working for Honeywell across multiple business models, sectors, geographic locations, and economic cycles.
- "The adoption of Accelerator and standardisation of global business models to enable maximal performance in each business segment" will be Kapur's primary areas of attention as CEO.

Viacom18 announces former captain MS Dhoni as their brand ambassador

- Viacom18 has appointed MS Dhoni as its brand ambassador to promote digital sports viewing. Dhoni will collaborate with Viacom18 to encourage fans to watch their favorite sports on digital platforms.
- He will participate in various network initiatives and feature in JioCinema's upcoming TATA IPL campaign, along with promoting the brand on his social media accounts.

Deepak Mohanty appointed as PFRDA chairman, Mamta Shankar as Whole-Time Member

- The Indian government has appointed Deepak Mohanty as the new chairman of Pension Fund Regulatory and Development Authority (PFRDA), replacing Supratim Bandyopadhyay whose term ended in January.

- Mohanty, a former executive director of Reserve Bank of India (RBI), previously served as a member of PFRDA.
- Additionally, Mamta Shankar has been appointed as the new whole-time member (Economics) for a period of three years or until she attains the age of 62 years, or until further orders.

G Krishnakumar appoints as Bharat Petroleum Corporation's chairman

- Bharat Petroleum Corporation Limited (BPCL), a 'Maharatna' and a Fortune Global 500 Company, announced that G. Krishnakumar has taken over as the Chairman and Managing Director of the company.
- Krishnakumar, an electrical and electronics engineer from National Institute of Technology, Tiruchirappalli and a postgraduate in finance management from Jamnalal Bajaj Institute of Management Studies, Mumbai, was executive director in the company before his elevation.
- He replaces Arun Kumar Singh, who retired as chairman in October 2022.
- Post that, Gupta was holding additional charge of the chairman. Krishnakumar will hold the position of chairman and managing director till April 2025 or until any further notice, whichever is earlier, according to an official order.

FSIB suggests Ashwani Kumar name as MD and CEO of UCO Bank

- The Financial Services Institutions Bureau (FSIB) has suggested that Ashwani Kumar, an executive director at Indian Bank, be appointed as the managing director of UCO Bank.
- Kumar has previously held positions at several other public sector banks, including Bank of Baroda, Corporation Bank, Oriental Bank of Commerce, and Punjab National Bank (PNB).
- The FSIB interviewed 11 candidates from various PSBs for the role of MD & CEO.
- The final decision on the appointment will be made by the Appointments Committee of the Cabinet led by Prime Minister Narendra Modi.

Luxor Selects Virat Kohli as Brand Ambassador

- Luxor Writing Instruments Pvt Ltd, a stationery manufacturer, has appointed renowned cricketer Virat Kohli as its latest brand ambassador.
- Kohli is widely regarded as one of the best cricketers of all time, having set numerous records throughout his career.

- He will represent Luxor's stationery products and help the company increase its appeal among young writers, thereby enhancing its position as a prominent writing instrument provider in the country.

Jayanti Chauhan to lead Bisleri after TCPL withdraws acquisition plan

- After Tata Consumer Products Ltd (TCPL) withdrew from acquiring Bisleri International, Ramesh Chauhan, the chairman of the company, announced that his daughter Jayanti Chauhan will now lead the bottled water company.
- He also stated that he has no intention of selling the business and is not currently in talks with any parties about doing so.
- Jayanti Chauhan is currently the vice chairperson of Bisleri and has been involved with the business for several years.
- She has been driving innovation and overseeing sales and marketing teams, with a focus on market penetration and brand value.
- TCPL confirmed that it has ceased negotiations with Bisleri and has not entered into any agreements for the acquisition.

Manmeet K Nanda appointed as MD & CEO of Invest India

- Manmeet K Nanda has been appointed as the new Managing Director and Chief Executive Officer of Invest India, a prestigious organization.
- The Ministry of Commerce and Industry has released a statement announcing the approval of Nanda's appointment by Invest India's board, following Deepak Bagla's decision to step down.
- Nanda was previously serving as the Joint Secretary in the Department for Promotion of Industry and Internal Trade (DPIIT).
- Bagla resigned from his post last week, leading to the need for a new MD and CEO at Invest India.

Arnab Banerjee named as MD & CEO of CEAT

- CEAT, the tyre manufacturer, has named Arnab Banerjee as its new Managing Director (MD) and Chief Executive Officer (CEO) following the resignation of Anant Goenka.
- Banerjee's term as MD and CEO will commence from April 1, 2023 and last for two years, according to the company's corporate filing.
- Anant Goenka will step down from his position as MD and CEO at the end of business hours on March 31, 2023, and will take on the role of non-executive

non-independent director and Vice Chairman of the company, subject to approval from members and other relevant authorities.

Salima Tete appointed as the AHF Athletes Ambassador

- National women's hockey team midfielder Salima Tete has appointed the AHF Athletes Ambassador from India for a term of two years.
- Tete accepted the certificate and the position during the Asian Hockey Federation (AHF) Congress in Mungyeong, Korea. Tete, who led the Indian women's junior hockey team to a fourth-place finish at the 2021 FIH Women's Junior World Cup in Potchefstroom, South Africa, is among four players from Asia to be appointed for the position.

Pranav Haridasan to be new MD and CEO of Axis Securities

- Pranav Haridasan has been appointed as the new Managing Director and Chief Executive Officer of Axis Securities for the next three years.
- B Gopkumar, who is currently the MD & CEO of Axis Securities, has been transferred to Axis Asset Management Company as MD & CEO.
- Pranav Haridasan has been appointed as the new Managing Director and Chief Executive Officer of Axis Securities for the next three years.
- He is currently serving as Managing Director and Co-Head of Equities at Axis Capital, and has over 20 years of experience in financial markets, having worked with Citigroup Global Markets as Director and Head of India/ ASEAN Execution Services before joining Axis Capital.

NDTV appoints former SEBI Chairman UK Sinha and Dipali Goenka as Independent Directors

- NDTV announced to the stock exchanges that Upendra Kumar Sinha, the former chairman of Securities Exchange Board of India (SEBI), has been appointed as the non-executive chairperson and independent director of the NDTV board of directors.
- Additionally, Dipali Goenka, the CEO of Welspun India, has also been appointed as an independent director on the NDTV board.

SpiceJet's Ajay Singh takes over as ASSOCHAM President

- Ajay Singh, the chief of SpiceJet, has become the new President of the Associated Chambers of Commerce and Industry of India (ASSOCHAM).

- He has replaced Sumant Sinha, who completed his tenure as Managing Director of Renew Power. Sanjay Nayar, the Founder and Chairman of Sorin Investment Fund, has been appointed as the new Senior Vice-President of ASSOCHAM.

Hero Motocorp Board appoints Niranjan Gupta as CEO

- The Board of Hero MotoCorp announced the appointment of Niranjan Gupta as the new Cheif Executive Officer (CEO) of the company, effective from May 1.
- Gupta, who currently serves as the CFO and Head of Strategy and M&A, will be elevated to the new role.
- Meanwhile, Pawan Munjal will remain the Executive Chairman and Whole-time Director on the Board.

Tata Power approves re-appointment of Praveer Sinha as CEO and MD

- Tata Power has re-appointed Praveer Sinha as the company's Chief Executive Officer (CEO) and Managing Director.
- His re-appointment to the top post is for a period of four years from May 1, 2023, to April 30, 2027, subject to the approval of members of the company, Tata Power said in a regulatory filing.
- His present tenure as CEO and MD is scheduled to conclude on April 30, 2023.

Star Sports signed Bollywood actor Ranveer Singh as its brand ambassador

- Star Sports, which is owned by The Walt Disney Company India, has appointed Bollywood actor Ranveer Singh as its brand ambassador.
- This is a significant step for the brand as it seeks to tap into Singh's immense popularity and love for sports to reach a wider and more diverse audience that may not have previously engaged deeply with sports.
- Singh will act as the "sutradhaar" or narrator for the upcoming season of the Indian Premier League (IPL), which the company is branding as the "Incredible League".
- He will also participate in creating content for the IPL, which is scheduled to begin on March 31st.

Manmeet K Nanda appointed as MD & CEO of Invest India

- Manmeet K Nanda has been appointed as the new Managing Director and Chief Executive Officer of Invest India, a prestigious organization.

- The Ministry of Commerce and Industry has released a statement announcing the approval of Nanda's appointment by Invest India's board, following Deepak Bagla's decision to step down.
- Nanda was previously serving as the Joint Secretary in the Department for Promotion of Industry and Internal Trade (DPIIT).
- Bagla resigned from his post last week, leading to the need for a new MD and CEO at Invest India.

NDTV appoints former SEBI Chairman UK Sinha and Dipali Goenka as Independent Directors

- NDTV announced to the stock exchanges that Upendra Kumar Sinha, the former chairman of Securities Exchange Board of India (SEBI), has been appointed as the non-executive chairperson and independent director of the NDTV board of directors.
- Additionally, Dipali Goenka, the CEO of Welspun India, has also been appointed as an independent director on the NDTV board.

51-year old Elon Musk becomes most followed Twitter user

- Elon Musk, the CEO of Twitter, has achieved the highest number of followers on the platform, exceeding former US President Barack Obama, who held the record since 2020.
- According to Guinness World Records, Twitter has around 450 million monthly active users, and Elon Musk has accumulated more than 133 million followers, which accounts for about 30% of the platform's total users.
- Musk assumed the role of CEO of Twitter on October 27, 2022, with 110 million followers, and within five months, his followers increased to 133 million.
- Previously, he ranked third after Barack Obama and Justin Bieber in terms of the most followed Twitter users.

Ranks and Reports

Elon Musk reclaims to the top, becomes richest person on the planet again

- Elon Musk, CEO of Tesla, once again overtook the position of richest person in the world on February 28, according to a Bloomberg Billionaires Index report.
- The second-placed French business tycoon Bernard Arnault has a net worth of $185 billion, trailing Tesla CEO Elon Musk by $187 billion.

- With a net worth of $117 billion, Amazon Executive Chairman Jeff Bezos ranks third in terms of wealth.
- The strong increase in Tesla stock price, which rose to 92% in 2023 and outpaced the Nasdaq 100 rally so far in 2023, has been cited as the cause of the jump in Musk's wealth.
- The increase in the Nasdaq 100 Index so far this year is 11%

World Bank's Women, Business and the Law Report 2023

- Economic growth and strength are boosted by gender equality, according to the World Bank's Women, Business and the Law Report 2023.
- It increases labour force participation and results in a more effective allocation of resources.
- Women may engage more fully in the economy and realise their full potential when they have equal access to economic opportunities, which boosts productivity and growth.

Mumbai Ranks at 37th Place Globally in Price Growth in Luxury Housing

- Mumbai's jumped to rank 37 from 92 in a global list of movement in prices of luxury homes as the city saw a gain of 6.4 percent during the 2022 calendar year.
- Property consultant Knight Frank virtually released 'The Wealth Report 2023' in which Mumbai has ranked 37th.
- Knight Frank Report states that the value of the Prime International Residential Index (PIRI 100) which tracks the movement in luxury house prices across the world increased by 5.2 percent YoY (year-on-year) in 2022.

Uttarakhand's Rudraprayag, Tehri top landslide index: ISRO report

- Rudraprayag and Tehri the two districts in Uttarakhand are facing the highest risk of landslides, according to satellite data collected over the past two decades.
- Data collected by the Indian Space Research Organisation (ISRO) has highlighted that Rudraprayag and Tehri Garhwal are at the highest risk of facing landslides, having seen the highest number of landslide incidents in the past 20 years.

- Knight Frank, a global real estate consultancy, released its Wealth Report 2023, which provides insights into the trends and performance of the prime residential property market across the world.

- Among Indian respondents, the consultant said 88 per cent saw a rise in UHNWI's (ultra-high-net-worth individuals) wealth in 2022.
- Out of which 35 per cent respondents said that Indian UHNWIs saw an increase in their wealth in excess of 10 per cent last year.
- Going forward, the Indian respondents expect wealth of the ultra-wealthy to continue to increase in 2023.

India 8th most polluted country in the world: Swiss firm IQAir Report

- According to the 'Global Air Quality' study published by the Swiss company IQAir, India fell from the fifth to the eighth most polluted nation in the world in 2022.
- The research shows that the PM2.5 level in the most polluted Indian cities is 53.3. The two Indian cities that made the list of the most polluted cities in the world are Bhiwadi, which is a suburb of Delhi, and Delhi, which was not far behind at 92.6.
- At the same time, 39 out of 50 cities in the list of most polluted cities are from India.

SIPRI report 2023: India world's largest arms importer

- India is still the world's largest importer of military equipment, despite an 11% decline in arms purchases between 2013–17 and 2018–22, according to a study by the Stockholm International Peace Research Institute (SIPRI).
- The report is released at a time when India has intensified its efforts to become self-reliant in the defence manufacturing sector.
- This year's defence budget included about Rs 1 lakh crore for domestic purchases, compared to Rs 84,598 crore, Rs 70,221 crore, and Rs 51,000 crore in the three years prior.

Literacy rate in India: Bihar lowest at 61.8%, Kerala highest at 94%

- According to the data shared by the Ministry of Education, Bihar (61.8 %) has the lowest literacy, followed by Arunachal Pradesh (65.3 %) and Rajasthan (66.1 %).
- Kerala has the highest literacy rate in India at 94%, followed by Lakshadweep at 91.85% and Mizoram at 91.33%.
- The literacy rate in rural India is 67.77 per cent as compared to 84.11 per cent in urban India.

TIME list of World's Greatest Places of 2023 Released, 2 Indian Places Makes the list

India's Mayurbhanj and Ladakh, which have been chosen for their endangered tigers and historic temples, as well as their adventures and cuisine, respectively, are two of the 50 locations which are featured in the TIME Magazine's list of World's Greatest Places in 2023.

QS Rankings: IIT-Delhi enters list of top 50 institutions for engineering

- The Indian Institute of Technology-Delhi has been ranked among the top 50 engineering institutions in the QS World University Rankings by Subject 2023.
- Additionally, this year, a total of 44 programmes offered by Indian higher education institutions in various disciplines have been ranked in the top 100 globally.
- This represents an increase from last year's report, which saw 35 Indian programmes listed in the top 100.

Hurun Global Rich List: India ranks third in terms of self-made billionaires

- According to the 2023 M3M Hurun Global Rich List, India is ranked third in terms of the number of billionaires. However, China has almost five times more billionaires than India.
- The list shows that India has 105 self-made billionaires, ranking third in this category. The combined wealth of these billionaires is $381 billion, according to the Hurun list.
- India's proportion of the world's billionaires has been consistently rising over the past five years, and it now accounts for 8% of the total global billionaire population, compared to 4.9% five years ago. Among these billionaires, 57% are self-made.

Science and Technology News

ISRO successfully tests cryogenic engine of its rocket for the moon mission

- The CE-20 cryogenic engine, which will power the nation's rocket for the third moon mission, Chandrayaan-3, had a flight acceptance hot test that was successfully completed, according to the Indian Space Research Organisation (ISRO).
- The LVM3-M4 rocket's cryogenic upper stage will be powered by the CE-20 cryogenic engine, according to the space agency.

- On February 24, a 25-second hot test was performed at the ISRO Propulsion Complex in Mahendragiri, Tamil Nadu

SpaceX launches NASA Crew-6 mission

- SpaceX launched NASA's Crew-6 mission to orbit en route to the International Space Station, with a Russian cosmonaut and United Arab Emirates astronaut joining two NASA crewmates for the flight.
- The SpaceX launch vehicle, consisting of a Falcon 9 rocket topped with an autonomously operated Crew Dragon capsule called Endeavour, lifted off at 12:34 a.m. EST (0534 GMT) from NASA's Kennedy Space Center in Cape Canaveral, Florida.

Scientists confirm existence of a fifth layer in Earth's core

- Researchers trying to uncover the secrets of Earth's geology have revealed the fifth layer of the planet.
- Seismic waves generated by earthquakes have revealed new insights about the deepest parts of Earth's inner core. The fifth layer is made of iron and nickel, the same materials that comprise the rest of the inner core.
- The team of researchers from the Australian National University measured the speeds at which these seismic waves penetrate and pass through the Earth's inner core.
- The team believes that this has presented evidence of a distinct layer inside Earth known as the innermost inner core.
- The existence of an internal metallic ball within the inner core, the innermost inner core, was hypothesised about 20 years ago.

Reliance Life Sciences receives a gene therapy technology licence from IIT Kanpur

- Reliance Life Sciences Pvt Ltd has received a licence from the Indian Institute of Technology Kanpur for a gene therapy method that has the potential to treat a variety of genetic eye ailments.

- Reliance Life Sciences will further develop the gene treatment technology from IIT Kanpur into a native product. The science of molecular medicine has recently seen the emergence of gene therapy employing viral vectors as a powerful tool.

SpaceX launches 40 OneWeb internet satellites, lands rocket

- SpaceX launched a Falcon 9 rocket from Cape Canaveral Space Force Station with 40 more internet satellites for rival OneWeb, followed by the landing of the rocket's first stage booster back at the Florida spaceport.
- The two-stage Falcon 9 lifted off from Cape Canaveral Space Force Station in Florida at 2:13 p.m. EST (1913 GMT).
- The rocket's first stage came back to Earth right on schedule, touching down on a landing pad at Cape Canaveral about 7 minutes and 50 seconds after launch.

Svaya Robotics unveils India's first homegrown quadruped robot and exoskeleton

- Svaya Robotics, a Hyderabad-based company, has partnered with two DRDO labs, the Research and Development Establishment in Pune (R&DE) and Defence Bio-engineering & Electro Medical Laboratory in Bengaluru (DEBEL), to create India's first quadruped robot and wearable exo-skeleton.
- The company has designed both robots to serve multiple purposes in industries and healthcare, and they are dual-use robots.

Google Bard: Everything you should know about

- It is built on Transformer technology, which is also the backbone of ChatGPT and other AI bots.
- Transformer technology was pioneered by Google and made open source in 2017.
- Transformer technology is a Neural Network Architecture, which is capable of making predictions based on inputs and is primarily used in natural language processing and computer vision technology.

- The architecture determines how the network processes information and influences its accuracy and efficiency in solving a particular problem. Common architectures include feedforward networks, recurrent networks, and convolutional neural networks.

Adobe launches generative 'Sensei GenAI' to transform customer experiences

- During the 'Adobe Summit', software giant Adobe unveiled new generative AI advancements in its Experience Cloud that seek to revolutionize the way companies provide customer experiences.
- Adobe customers can effortlessly switch between Sensei GenAI services and current features within their workflows while using Adobe Experience Cloud, according to the company's statement.

Microsoft introduces 'Bing Image Creator' powered by OpenAI's DALL-E

- In the latest preview of Bing and Edge, Microsoft has added a new functionality called 'Bing Image Creator', which enables users to generate an image based on their written description by utilizing an enhanced version of Open AI's DALL-E model.
- Microsoft has announced the deployment of Bing Image Creator to Bing preview users via Bing chat, as well as the availability of the feature in Microsoft Edge for both desktop and mobile users worldwide in English.

Surge in Covid-19 cases in India linked to highly contagious XBB1.16 variant

- India has seen a surge in daily Covid-19 infections, with 349 cases of the newly detected XBB1.16 variant, which may be responsible for the recent increase in cases.
- According to data from the Indian SARS-CoV-2 Genomics Consortium (INSACOG), Maharashtra has the highest number of XBB1.16 variant cases with 105 cases, followed by Telangana with 93 cases, Karnataka with 61 cases, and Gujarat with 54 cases.

- The XBB1.16 variant, which is considered to be the most contagious variant so far, is a recombinant lineage of the virus and a descendant of the XBB lineage of Covid-19. It was first detected in India in January 2022, when two samples tested positive for the variant. In February, 140 XBB1.16 variant samples were reported, and in March, 207 XBB1.16 variant samples were found.

NASA and ISRO have jointly manufactured an earth science satellite named, NISAR

- Dr. Jitendra Singh, the Union Minister of State for Science & Technology, announced in the Rajya Sabha that NASA and ISRO have collaboratively built an earth science satellite called NISAR (NASA-ISRO Synthetic Aperture Radar).

- The satellite's primary objectives are to design, develop, and launch a dual-frequency (L and S band) radar imaging satellite, and to explore new application areas using L & S Band microwave data, particularly in surface deformation studies, terrestrial biomass structure, natural resource mapping and monitoring, and research on the dynamics of ice-sheets, glaciers, forests, oil slicks, etc.

Sports News

Manchester United won the Carabao Cup title 2023

- Manchester United ended their 6-year trophy drought when they defeated Newcastle United 2-0 to win the Carabao Cup in Wembley. The final battle was fought between Manchester United and Newcastle. Manchester United is winning the trophy after six years. Newcastle is a Saudi Arabia-backed club.
- The Carabao cup is also called the EFL cup. It is a major football trophy played in England. More than 92 clubs participate in the knockout competition.
- In 2023, the trophy was won by Manchester United. Liverpool is the most successful club in the competition. The team has won more than nine championships. (Carabao is an energy drink in Thailand).
- Winning the Carabao cup is essential to enter the UEFA Champions League. Apart from winning the Carabao cup, the team should also finish the Premier League in the top four.

Jaipur to get India's 2nd largest cricket stadium named after Anil Agarwal

- Vedanta's Hindustan Zinc Limited (HZL) has signed a Memorandum of Understanding (MoU) with the Rajasthan Cricket Association to build the world's third-largest cricket stadium in Chonp village, Jaipur.
- This project involves an investment of INR 300 crore, making it one of the largest corporate investments in India's sports infrastructure.
- The stadium will be named the Anil Agarwal International Cricket Stadium, Jaipur.
- The objective of the workshop is to establish a policy framework and practices that ensure the scientific implementation of Human Factors Engineering (HFE) in the defence sector, thus contributing to the vision of 'Aatmanirbhar Bharat.'

Jeswin Aldrin Breaks National Record at AFI National Jumps Competition

- Tamil Nadu's Jeswin Aldrin broke the national record in the men's long jump in the second AFI National Jumps Competition.
- Jeswin Aldrin, 21-year-old, leaped 8.42 meters to take over the previous mark of 8.36 meters set by India teammate M Sreeshankar at the Federation Cup in Kozhikode in April 2022.
- Aldrin previously won silver at the Asian Indoor Championships in Astana last month with a 7.97-meter jump and made the most of being in a competitive frame to break the national record.

India's Triple-Jumper Aishwarya Babu Banned by NADA for Four Years

- India's top triple-jumper Aishwarya Babu has been banned by the National Anti-Doping Agency's (NADA) disciplinary panel for four years for using a prohibited anabolic steroid.
- Aishwarya Babu, 25 years old, was dropped from the Birmingham Commonwealth Games in 2022, along with sprinter S Dhanalakshmi after testing positive for the steroid, which is on the World Anti-Doping Agency's (WADA) prohibited list.
- Aishwarya has been given time till 6th March 2023 to file an appeal against the ban after receiving the ban notice from NADA's Appeal Panel on 13th February 2023.

Asian Chess Federation confers D Gukesh with 2023 award

- Indian Grandmaster D Gukesh has been honoured with 2023 award by the Asian Chess Federation (ACF) for clinching the gold medal with a record-breaking score of 9/11 in the 44th Chess Olympiad at Mahabalipuram.
- Gukesh became only the sixth Indian to break the 2700 Elo-rating mark, and the youngest Grandmaster from the country to be rated above 2700.
- The All India Chess Federation (AICF) bagged the 'Most Active Federation' award conferred during the ACF annual summit, which is underway her.

Karnataka end 54-years wait, wins Santosh Trophy

- Karnataka ended their 54-year wait to win the Santosh Trophy national football championship, beating Meghalaya 3-2 in a pulsating final at the King Fahd International Stadium in the Saudi Arabia capital.
- Services beat Punjab 2-0 in the playoff to finish third. PP Shafeel and Christopher Kamei scored in either half. Services, winners of five of the last 10 editions, took the lead in the seventh minute through a strike from distance by Shafeel before Kamei converted a left-footed attempt from outside the box.
- Karnataka (Sunil Kumar 2′, Bekley Oram 19′, Robin Yadav 42′) 3 – 2 Meghalaya (Brolington Warlarpih 19′, Sheen Stevenson Sphktung 60′).

Max Verstappen wins season-opening Bahrain Grand Prix 2023

- Max Verstappen won the season-opening Bahrain Grand Prix from pole position, leading almost the entire race as he opened the defense of his back-to-back Formula One titles.
- It was the first time he had won in Bahrain and also the first time he had triumphed in a Formula One opener.
- Red Bull also clinched a dominant 1-2 with Sergio Perez finishing second while 41-year-old Fernando Alonso took a brilliant third place and claimed a 99th career podium on a stunning race debut for Aston Martin.

Irani Cup 2022-23 final: Rest of India crowned champions

- In the final of the Irani Cup 2022-23, Team Rest of India secured their 30th title win in the Indian domestic tournament, continuing their dominant performance.
- They defeated Madhya Pradesh by 238 runs. Yashasvi Jaiswal, who showcased brilliant batting skills across both innings, was adjudged the Player of the Match.
- He smashed a double century and a century in the two innings, contributing significantly to ROI's victory.

Former Australia Cricket Captain Tim Paine Announces Retirement from the Sport

- Tim Paine, the former captain of the Australian test cricket team, has announced his retirement from cricket after playing his last Sheffield Shield first-class match for Tasmania against Queensland.
- Paine led the Australian team in 23 tests from 2018 to 2021 and played a total of 35 tests in his career.
- He took over as captain after Steve Smith was stripped of the role following the ball-tampering scandal during Australia's 2018 tour of South Africa.

Pankaj Advani retains Asian Billiards title defeating Damani

- Pankaj Advani, the Indian cue sports champion, has retained his Asian Billiards title in the 100-up format after defeating his compatriot Brijesh Damani 5-1 in the final held at Qatar Billiards and Snooker Federation (QBSF) Academy.
- Advani, who has won the International Billiards and Snooker Federation (IBSF) world championship 25 times, won the match with a scoreline of 100(51)-18, 100(88)-9, 86(54)-101(75), 100-26, 100(66)-2, 101(64)-59.

IPL India's first unicorn with a $1.1 billion valuation: D&P report

- D&P Advisory has analyzed the Indian Premier League (IPL) and reported that the cricket tournament was India's first unicorn, with a valuation of $1.1 billion in 2008, the year it was launched.
- The advisory had previously announced that IPL had become a decacorn (valued at $10.9 billion) recently. D&P Advisory is now preparing to publish a new analysis called "IPL: The Pioneer of Indian Unicorns."

WPL 2023 Final: Mumbai Indians defeated Delhi Capitals by seven wickets

- In the Women's Premier League (WPL) 2023 final, held at the Brabourne Stadium in Mumbai, the Mumbai Indians won against the Delhi Capitals by seven wickets.
- The Delhi Capitals chose to bat first after winning the toss, and set a target of 132 runs.
- In response, the Mumbai Indians achieved the target by scoring 134/3 in 19.3 overs.

- Nat Sciver-Brunt played exceptionally well and remained unbeaten after scoring 60 runs off 55 balls, while the team's captain Harmanpreet Kaur contributed 37 runs off 39 balls.
- The Harmapreet Kaur-led side scripted history by becoming the winners of the 2023 edition of the tournament.

2023 IBA Women's World Boxing Championships: Check the list of Winners

- India emerged as a dominant force at the 13th edition of the IBA Women's World Boxing Championship 2023, held in New Delhi.
- The event concluded with four Indian female boxers securing gold medals in different weight categories.
- Saweety Boora, Nitu Ghanghas, Nikhat Zareen, and Lovlina Borgohain were the top performers in their respective categories, contributing to India's historic success in the competition.
- This was the second time India achieved such a remarkable feat, the first being in the 2006 event.
- The 13th edition of the Women's World Boxing Championship 2023 was organised by the International Boxing Association (IBA) and took place from March 15 to March 26, 2023.

Shakib Al Hasan surpasses Southee to become the top T20I wicket-taker

- Shakib Al Hasan has surpassed Tim Southee to become the leading wicket-taker in T20I cricket during the second T20I match against Ireland in Chattogram.
- With 136 wickets in T20I at an average of 20.67 and an economy rate of 6.8, Shakib is considered as one of the best all-rounders in T20 cricket.
- He has also scored 2339 runs at a strike rate of 122.33 in T20I.
- Shakib made his debut in T20I against Zimbabwe in 2006 and has played 114 matches since then, featuring in all seven editions of the ICC Men's T20 World Cup.

Sir Alex Ferguson and Arsene Wenger inducted into Premier League Hall of Fame

- On March 29, the Premier League inducted former Manchester United manager Sir Alex Ferguson and ex-Arsenal boss Arsene Wenger into its Hall of Fame.
- This is the first time that managers have been included in this prestigious list.

- The two managers had a fierce rivalry during the 1990s, with a combined 16 English top-flight titles to their names.
- Ferguson led Manchester United to 13 Premier League titles during his 26-year reign, while Wenger won three Premier League titles and seven FA Cups with Arsenal during his 22-year tenure.
- The Premier League Hall of Fame was launched in 2021 to honour players who have made an exceptional contribution to the league.

National News

Pusa Krishi Vigyan Mela Organized by IARI in New Delhi

- The Pusa Krishi Vigyan Mela is organized every year by the Indian Agricultural Research Institute (IARI) and this year it will be held in New Delhi from 2nd to 4th March 2023.
- The Pusa Krishi Vigyan Mela will be inaugurated by the Chief Guest, Union Minister of Agriculture and Farmers Welfare, Narendra Singh Tomar.
- This time the theme of the fair is "Nutrition, Food and Environmental Protection with Shree Anna".

Nitin Gadkari Inaugurated 7 National Highway Projects in MP

- Union Minister for Road Transport and Highways Nitin Gadkari inaugurated 7 National Highway projects worth Rs 2,444 crore, totaling 204 km in Rewa, Madhya Pradesh.
- Union Minister Nitin Gadkari informed that with the construction of the Churhat tunnel and bypass, the length between Rewa to Sidhi has decreased by 7 km. Now instead of two and a half hours, people will be able to cover this distance in 45 minutes.
- The Minister informed that the movement of vehicles in the Rewa-Sidhi section will be facilitated by the construction of the tunnel, white tigers, and other wild animals, and the entire forest ecosystem will be protected.
- With the construction of the Devtalab-Naigarhi road, the connectivity of Rewa district with Prayagraj and Varanasi will be easy.

RBI's Data Centre And Cybersecurity Training Institute To Come Up In Bhubaneswar

- The Governor of the Reserve Bank of India (RBI), Shaktikanta Das, initiated the establishment of a "Greenfield Data Centre" and an "Enterprise Computing & Cybersecurity Training Institute" in Bhubaneswar, Odisha, during a foundation stone laying ceremony.
- The new Data Centre and Training Institute, which will cover an area of 18.55 acres, will be able to address the emerging needs of the RBI and the financial sector, according to a statement by the central bank.

'Catch the Rain 2023' campaign to be launched by President Murmu'

- The 'Catch the Rain 2023' campaign was introduced by President Droupadi Murmu in New Delhi. The campaign's central idea is the sustainability of drinking water sources.
- Addressing at the ceremony, the President stated that since India only has 4% of the world's water resources, water management and conservation are India's most pressing challenges.
- President Droupadi Murmu claimed that due to uncontrolled urbanisation, traditional methods of water conservation have been abandoned in the nation.
- The President emphasised that these issues—water scarcity and global warming—are consequences of it.

Swachhotsav: A 3-week Women Led Swachhata Campaign launched by MoHUA

- Union Housing and Urban Affairs Minister Hardeep Singh Puri launched 'Swachhotsav', a three-week women-led swachhata campaign under the Swachh Bharat Mission (Urban).
- Series of events and activities will be organized across cities to celebrate women from all walks of life.
- According to the ministry, at the launch, the first edition of Women Icons leading Sanitation and Waste Management (WINS) Challenge-2023 was also announced.

Ashok Leyland unveils all-women production line at Tamil Nadu plant

- Indian commercial vehicle manufacturer, Ashok Leyland, has launched an "All Women Production Line" with 100 per cent female employees at its Hosur plant in Tamil Nadu.
- The initiative to introduce an all-women production line is to promote women empowerment and encourage them take up roles in manufacturing industry.

Adani-Hindenburg Row: Supreme Court forms experts committee to look into Hindenburg report on Adani Group; Head AM Sapre

- The Supreme Court ordered an experts committee to be set up, headed by a retired Supreme Court judge, AM Sapre, after a batch of PILs was filed on the recent Adani Group shares crash triggered by the US-based short-seller Hindenburg Research's allegations of fraud.
- Meanwhile, the Supreme Court also told the Securities and Exchange Board of India (SEBI) to finish the probe into the Adani Group-Hindenburg saga within a period of two months.
- The Supreme Court bench, led by Chief Justice of India DY Chandrachud, has appointed six members as part of the expert committee. It includes OP Bhatt, Justice JP Devadhar, KV Kamath, Nandan Nilekani and Somasekhar Sundaresan, and will be headed by Former Supreme Court judge Justice AM Sapre.

PM Modi inaugurates world's longest railway platform in Hubballi, Karnataka

- Prime Minister Narendra Modi dedicated World`s longest railway platform of 1.5 kilometres at Sri Siddhaarooda railway station in Hubballi in the state of Karnataka.
- The inauguration of the platform was done during the PM's Karnataka visit in the presence of Union Minister Pralhad Joshi.
- It is to be noted that Indian Railways, South Western Railway Zones Hubbali is now registered in the Guinness Book of World Records for having the longest platform.

Union Home Ministry announced 10% reservation for former Agniveers

- The Union home ministry has announced a 10 per cent reservation for former Agniveers in vacancies in the Central Industrial Security Force (CISF), just after taking a similar initiative for jobs for them in the BSF.
- Government also amended the rules of the Border Security Force (BSF) and brought in similar changes.

Nitin Gadkari unveiled first methanol run buses in Bengaluru

- The first methanol-powered buses in Bengaluru will be unveiled by Union Minister for Road and Transport, Nitin Gadkari.
- The Bengaluru Metropolitan Transport Corporation (BMTC), NITI Aayog, Indian Oil Company (IOC), and Ashok Leyland are working together to carry out the initiative, which aims to lower the level of pollutants.
- A top BMTC official informed that MD15 (diesel with 15% methanol) bus pilot testing will begin around 5:30 pm from Vidhana Soudha.
- The BMTC intends to launch 80 buses that will use methanol fuel as part of the trial project, and 20 Ashok Leyland buses will also be introduced in the first stages.
- The Indian Oil Company will offer free fuel and methanol for three months as part of the experiment.

India's bullet train to run by August 2026: Railway Minister

- According to railways and telecom minister Ashwini Vaishnaw, the first bullet train in India will begin service in August 2026. The project will stimulate the economy because several of the suppliers to the project have begun receiving export orders.
- The government intends to start operating the first bullet train in August 2026. The goal is to run the bullet train on a larger section in 2027.
- The Indian railways is building the country's first bullet train from Ahmedabad, Gujarat to Mumbai, Maharashtra over 508-kilometer route.

Atal Innovation Mission launches ATL Sarthi

- Atal Innovation Mission is establishing Atal Tinkering Laboratories (ATLs) in schools across India to foster curiosity, creativity, and imagination in young minds; and inculcate skills such as design thinking mindset, computational thinking, adaptive learning, physical computing, etc. As of date, AIM has funded 10,000 schools to establish Atal Tinkering Labs (ATLs).
- AIM is continuously strengthening this ecosystem by developing tools and frameworks to enhance the performance of ATLs and achieve the desired objectives. ATL Sarthi is one such initiative in this direction. As the name suggests, Sarthi is a charioteer and ATL Sarthi will enable the ATLs to be efficient and effective.

AAHAR 2023: Asia's biggest International Food and Hospitality Fair begins in Delhi

- The objective of Aahar 2023, which was put together with the help of the Union Ministry of Food Processing Industries, the Agriculture and Processed Food Produacts Export Development Authority (APEDA), and other organisations, is to showcase the hospitality industry's potential and showcase technologies, goods, and services to both domestic and foreign consumers.
- The greatest four-day culinary event in India is called Aahar 2023, where whole-salers, caterers, hoteliers, and restaurant owners gather to source the best food, hospitality, and equipment as well as to assess industry trends.
- At the fair's major event, Culinary Art India, WACS-certified jury members from India and overseas will also assess the skill of more than 500 cooks.

Narender Singh Tomar inaugurates "AgriUnifest" in Bengaluru

- Union Minister of Agriculture and Farmers Welfare Narendra Singh Tomar on 15 March 2023, inaugurated "AgriUnifest" in Bengaluru, Karnataka.
- It is a 5-day cultural program, organized by Bangalore Agricultural University in collaboration with the Indian Council of Agricultural Research (ICAR).
- More than 2500 students from 60 State Universities/Central Universities have participated.

Indian Railways to become Net Zero Carbon Emitter by 2030

- Indian Railways has set a target of becoming a 'net-zero carbon emitter' by 2030, said Union Railways Minister Ashwini Vaishnaw in a written reply to the Lok Sabha.
- The Railways plans to achieve this ambitious target in two steps: A complete transition to electric trains by December 2023 and powering the trains and stations primarily through non-renewable sources by 2030.

India aims at becoming 'Global Hub for Green Ship' building by 2030

- India is aiming to become a leader in the global shipbuilding industry by launching the Green Tug Transition Programme (GTTP) and setting a goal of becoming a 'Global Hub for Green Ship' building by 2030.
- The GTTP will start with the production of Green Hybrid Tugs, which will run on Green Hybrid Propulsion systems, and eventually switch to alternative fuel sources like Methanol, Ammonia, and Hydrogen.

- Union Minister of Ports, Shipping & Waterways (MoPSW) and Ayush, Shri Sarbananda Sonowal has inauguarted the National Centre of Excellence in Green Port & Shipping (NCoEGPS) set-up in Gurugram, Haryana, and the Green Tugs will begin operating in major ports by 2025.

PM Modi inaugurates new ITU Area Office and Innovation Center in New Delhi

- On March 22, the Prime Minister of India, Narendra Modi, inaugurated the International Telecommunication Union (ITU) Area Office and Innovation Centre in the country.
- At an event held in New Delhi, he also launched the Bharat 6G Vision Document, as well as the 6G Research and Development Test Bed and the Call Before U dig App.
- ITU, a specialized agency of the United Nations for information and communication technologies, has its headquarters in Geneva and operates a vast network of regional, field, and area offices.

Govt approves installation of 'Statue of Knowledge' dedicated to Ambedkar

- On April 13, a 70-feet tall statue of Dr. Babasaheb Ambedkar will be unveiled in Latur city, Maharashtra.
- The unveiling ceremony will take place in the presence of Union ministers Kiren Rijiju and Ramdas Athawale, along with other dignitaries such as former Maharashtra chief minister Devendra Fadnavis and state minister Sanjay Bansode.

Will SVB collapse impact the Indian talent market?

- Startups that had built their reserves and deposits at SVB are likely to be affected by the bank's collapse, and efforts are underway to secure and recover their reserves.
- For these startups, the main inconvenience will be a reduction in liquidity and delays in accessing funds.
- However, they have a means of resolving the situation and are unlikely to resort to layoffs. They may need to exercise short-term austerity measures to navigate through this period.

Indian Government Launches DigiClaim Platform for Farmer Insurance Claims

- The Agriculture Minister of India, Narendra Singh Tomar, has introduced a new platform called 'DigiClaim' on the national crop insurance portal.
- This platform is aimed at expediting the disbursement of insurance claims to farmers who have availed themselves of crop insurance.
- To demonstrate its effectiveness, the Minister used the platform to transfer a total insurance claim of Rs. 1,260.35 crore to insured farmers in several Indian states, including Rajasthan, Uttar Pradesh, Himachal Pradesh, Chhattisgarh, Uttarakhand, and Haryana, with just a single click.

Sarbananda Sonowal inaugurates 'Sagar Manthan', the Real-time Performance Monitoring Dashboard of MoPSW

- The Real-time Performance Monitoring Dashboard of MoPSW called 'Sagar Manthan' was virtually launched by Union Minister for Ports, Shipping and Waterways and Ayush Shri Sarbananda Sonowal.
- The digital platform is designed to have all integrated data related to the ministry and other subsidiaries.

Amit Shah inaugurated Vedic Heritage portal in New Delhi

- Union Home Minister Amit Shah inaugurated the Vedic Heritage portal in New Delhi.
- The primary aim of the portal is to communicate the messages enshrined in the Vedas and make it more accessible to the common people.
- According to Union Culture Minister G Kishan Reddy, the Vedic Heritage portal now has audio-visual recordings of the four Vedas.
- These recordings contain over 18,000 mantras of the four Vedas, with a total duration of over 550 hours.

PM Modi launched 'Call Before u Dig' app

- Prime Minister Modi has recently launched an app called "Call Before You Dig" to prevent uncoordinated digging that can cause damage to underground utility assets, such as optical fibre cables.
- The app has been developed jointly by the Department of Telecommunications and the Bhaskaracharya Institute for Space Applications and Geoinformatics, which operates under the Gujarat government.
- Its primary aim is to protect the country's underground public infrastructure.

Amit Shah unveils the statues of Lord Basaveshwara and Nadaprabhu Kempegowda in Bengaluru

- Union Home Minister and Minister of Cooperation Shri Amit Shah unveiled the statues of Lord Basaveshwara ji and Nadaprabhu Kempegowda ji at the State Assembly premises in Bengaluru, Karnataka.
- Lord Basaveshwara and Nadaprabhu Kempegowda are two prominent historical figures from Karnataka, a state in southern India.
- These statues will continue to give Basavanna ji and Kempegowda ji's message of social justice, democracy, good governance and development to those who get elected in the assembly.

India's highways infra to match US by 2024

- According to Nitin Gadkari, India's Union Road Transport and Highways Minis ter, the country's highways infrastructure will be at par with that of the United States by 2024.
- He revealed that the government is working on this goal in a time-bound 'mission mode,' which includes the development of green expressways and rail over bridges.
- These initiatives are aimed at ensuring that India's highway infrastructure matches the standards of the US by the specified timeline.

PM Modi inaugurated Whitefield (Kadugodi) for Krishnarajapura Metro Line

- The Whitefield (Kadugodi) to Krishnarajapura Metro Line was inaugurated by Prime Minister Narendra Modi, who expressed his happiness in a tweet.
- He mentioned that this new metro line will enhance the 'Ease of Living' for the people of Bengaluru, by improving transportation and connectivity in the region.
- The Prime Minister launched the 13.71 km extension project of Reach-1 under Bangalore Metro Phase 2, which runs up to Krishnarajapura Metro Line.
- The project was completed at an estimated cost of around Rs 4250 crores.

India's First Quantum Computing-based Telecom Network Link Now Operational: Ashwini Vaishnaw

- India's first quantum computing-based telecom network link has been made operational between Sanchar Bhawan and National Informatics Centre office in New Delhi.

- Telecom Minister Ashwini Vaishnaw announced prize money of Rs 10 lakh for ethical hackers who can break the encryption of the system and also launched a hackathon challenge for anyone who can break the system developed by C-DoT, with a reward of Rs 10 lakh per break.

"Swachhotsav 2023- 1000 Cities are targeted to become 3-Star Garbage Free by October 2024"

- During the International Zero Waste Day 2023 in New Delhi, Sh. Hardeep S. Puri, The Hon'ble Minister for Housing and Urban Affairs, announced that 1000 cities are targeted to achieve a 3-Star Garbage Free rating by October 2024.
- The GFC-Star rating protocol, launched in January 2018 to promote a competitive and mission-driven approach among ULBs, has seen a significant increase in certification since its inception.
- The Minister commended the 'Swachhta Doots' from all over the country, praising them for being agents of change and leaders in their communities, as well as for their ability to turn challenges into opportunities for livelihood.

States News

Salhoutuonuo Kruse and Hekani Jakhalu become 1st women MLAs from Nagaland

- Salhoutuonuo Kruse and Hekani Jakhalu, both from the ruling Nationalist Democratic Progressive Party, made history by becoming the first women candidates to be elected in the state assembly election.
- In a significant milestone, people in Nagaland have elected two women candidates after 60 years since it attained statehood. Kruse won from Western Angami AC and Jakhalu.

Assembly Election Results 2023, BJP Held Power of Tripura and Nagaland

- As the counting of votes for the Assembly Election Results 2023 has been done, the BPJ took the lead and crossed the halfway mark in both Tripura and Nagaland.
- In Tripura, Manik Saha will be the Chief Minister and serve his second term, he defeated the veteran Congress leader Ashish Kumar Saha with a margin of 1,257 votes.

- Prime Minister Narendra Modi is likely to address the BJP workers and supporters as the party retained power successfully in Tripura.

Uttarakhand CM Dhami announced the launch of self-employment scheme for single women

- Chief Minister of Uttarakhand, Pushkar Singh Dhami has announced the launch of Mukhyamantri Ekal Mahila Swarozgar Yojana in the state at the end of Women Empowerment and Safety Week.
- Women in remote villages of the state are giving impetus to the rural economy through self-help groups. Through their skill potential, women are providing strength to the economy of their families.
- The Chief Minister said that under the leadership of Prime Minister Narendra Modi, many efforts have been made to empower the mother power.

Ashwini Vaishnaw releases 'Go Green, Go Organic' cover for Sikkim

- Union Minister Ashwini Vaishnaw and four Sikkim ministers released a unique cover of the Department of Posts, 'Go Green, Go Organic' for Sikkim.
- The union minister thanked Department of Posts for this release and congratulated Sikkim State for its achievements of becoming the first state of the world to get recognized as an Organic state by the World Book of Records (London).

Attukal Pongala celebrated with pomp by women in Kerala

- Thousands of women devotees gathered at the Attukal Bhagavathy temple on March 7 for Attukal Pongala, the ninth day of the annual 10-day women-centric festival.
- 300 priests have been appointed for the sanctification ceremony at 2.30 pm and the city of Thiruvananthapuram is in a very festive mood.
- The day started at 10.30 am when thousands of women across Thiruvananthapuram lit their hearths with the fire of the 'Pandara Aduppu' at the Attukal Bhagavathy temple.
- This traditional gesture signifies the beginning of the annual Attukal Pongala ritual.

Manik Saha sworn in as 13th CM of Tripura

- Manik Saha took oath as 13th chief minister for the second time as Tripura Chief Minister after the BJP clinched a victory in the February 16 Assembly polls.

- Governor Satyadeo Narayan Arya administered the oath of office and secrecy to Mr. Saha and eight more MLAs as Ministers in the presence of Prime Minister Narendra Modi, Union Home Minister Amit Shah held a marathon meeting with TIPRA Motha chief Pradyot Bikram Manikya Debbarma and 13 MLAs of his party.
- Four of the new ministers have been retained from the previous government. The possible strength of the Council of Ministers in the 60-member House is 12.

Conrad Sangma sworn-in as Meghalaya Chief Minister for 2nd term

- Conrad Kongkal Sangma was sworn in as the Meghalaya chief minister for the second successive term in the presence of Prime Minister Narendra Modi.
- Governor Phagu Chauhan administered the oath of office to Sangma, along with his two deputies Prestone Tynsong and Sniawbhaland Dhar, and nine other ministers.
- Sangma won from the South Tura constituency with a margin of 5,016 against Bharatiya Janata Party's Bernard N Marak, as per the data shared by the Election Commission of India on March 2.

Manipur's Yaoshang festival begins

- Yaoshang, Manipur's version of Holi, which lasts for five days, has begun. On the full moon of Lamta (February–March) in the Meitei lunar calendar, the event is observed annually.
- Yaosang, sometimes referred to as the Burning of the Straw Hut, starts just after dusk and is immediately followed by Yaoshang. In a practise known as "nakatheng," kids solicit their neighbours for financial gifts.

Maharashtra to introduce 4th women's policy

- Deputy Chief Minister Devendra Fadanvis informed the Maharashtra's Legislative Council that the state will introduce the fourth women's policy to give more opportunities to women by considering the issues of women from all groups.
- On the occasion of International Women's Day, Deputy Speaker of the Legislative Council Neelam Gorhe tabled a proposal to provide equal and dignified positions to women in all sectors.
- While replying to the proposal, Mr Fadanvis said that apart from education, and employment, the women's policy will consider other important aspects, including economic empowerment and gender equality. He also announced that the

government will introduce a rehabilitation scheme for those above 18 years old girls from the orphanage.

A new initiative called 'beggar-free city' started in Nagpur, Maharashtra

- In Nagpur, Maharashtra, a new project known as "beggar-free city" has been launched. Amitesh Kumar, the Nagpur City commissioner of police, announced that notification 144 CrPC has been issued in this regard.
- The social welfare division of the Nagpur Municipal Corporation (NMC) and the Nagpur City Police are partners in this effort. In order to accommodate homeless people in its shelters, the NMC has developed particular provisions.

Uttarakhand govt approves 10 % horizontal reservation for statehood activists

- The decision on the reservation to Statehood activists assumes significance since the governor had returned the bill granting 10 per cent reservation to the statehood activists in the past. The statehood activists are not getting the benefit of reservation in government jobs for the past 12 years.
- The government of Uttarakhand has approved a 10% horizontal reservation for statehood campaigners in state government positions. Under the direction of Chief Minister Pushkar Singh Dhami, the decision was made during a cabinet meeting held in Bhararisain.

Asia's largest 4-metre liquid mirror telescope inaugurated in Uttarakhand

- Dr. Jitendra Singh, the Union Minister of State (Independent Charge) for Science & Technology, inaugurated Asia's largest 4-metre International Liquid Mirror Telescope at Devasthal, Uttarakhand, in the presence of Lt. Gen (Retd.) Gurmeet Singh, the Governor of Uttarakhand.
- The Aryabhatta Research Institute of Observational Sciences (ARIES) has declared that the 4-meter International Liquid Mirror Telescope (ILMT) is operational and can now be used to observe the deep celestial sky.
- The telescope recorded its first light in the second week of May 2022 and is located on the Devasthal Observatory campus of ARIES in the Nainital district of Uttarakhand.
- ARIES is an independent institute under the Department of Science and Technology (DST) of the Indian Government, situated at an altitude of 2450 meters.

'World Trade Center' To Come Up In Kolkata's Salt Lake: Merlin Group

- Merlin Group has partnered with the World Trade Centers Association to develop a World Trade Center in Kolkata that will cover an area of 3.5 million square feet.
- The project's License Agreement was signed by Scott Wang, Vice President of the World Trade Centers Association (WTCA) Asia Pacific region, and Merlin Group's Chairman, Sushil Mohta, and Managing Director, Saket Mohta.
- The project, which is being built in Salt Lake, West Bengal, is estimated to require an investment of approximately Rs 1,500 crore.
- The oldest World Trade Center in India is located in Mumbai, and there are additional Centers in Bangalore, Chennai, New Delhi, Noida, Pune, and other cities.

Himanta Biswa Sarma launches Mission Lifestyle for Environment(LiFE) in Assam

- Chief Minister of Assam, Himanta Biswa Sarma, inaugurated the 'Mission Lifestyle for Environment' (LiFE) in the state, which is a global mass movement led by Prime Minister Narendra Modi.
- Sarma stated that the initiative aims to encourage an environmentally conscious lifestyle, with a focus on utilizing resources rather than engaging in wasteful consumption.
- As part of the Mission Lifestyle for Environment (LiFE) initiative, various week-long activities will be conducted across all districts in Assam.
- These activities will target seven identified categories, including energy and water conservation, reducing plastic and e-waste, and promoting healthy lifestyles, according to Sarma.

Haldwani to get a sports university: Uttarakhand CM

- Uttarakhand Chief Minister Pushkar Singh Dhami has announced the government will set up a sports university in the Kumaun region's Haldwani town.
- Dhami, who made the announcement on the occasion of completion of one year of the formation of his government, said there had been longstanding demands from several sports associations for such a university.
- The international stadium of Haldwani will be upgraded into a sports university.

Tamil Nadu's 18th Wildlife Sanctuary Opens in Erode

- The government of Tamil Nadu has decided to declare Thanthai Periyar Wildlife Sanctuary as the 18th wildlife sanctuary in the state.

- This sanctuary covers an area of 80,567 hectares in the forest regions of Anthi yur and Gobichettipalayam taluks in Erode district, and includes reserve forest areas in Anthiyur, Bargur, Thattakarai, and Chennampatti.
- It is home to a variety of wild animals such as tigers, elephants, leopards, wild boars, gaurs, and deer.
- This wildlife sanctuary is located in close proximity to other sanctuaries such as Malai Mahadeshwara wildlife sanctuary, BRT Wildlife Sanctuary, Cauvery wildlife sanctuary in Karnataka, and it serves as a connecting point between Nilgiris Biosphere Reserve and Cauvery South Wildlife Sanctuary.
- This announcement was made during the state budget.

NGT slaps ₹10 crore penalty on Kerala government for failure to protect Ramsar sites

- The Kerala government has been fined Rs 10 crore by the Principal Bench of the National Green Tribunal (NGT) for their inability to prevent the uncontrolled pollution of the designated Ramsar sites.
- The order by NGT was made in lines with a petition alleging failure of statutory and administrative authorities in taking remedial action for protection of the Vembanad and Ashtamudi lakes hit by illegal waste dumping.

New species of Moray eel discovered off Cuddalore coast named after Tamil Nadu

- A team of scientists from thc Indian Council of Agricultural Research (ICAR) has discovered a new species of Moray Eel fish from the Cuddalore coast in Tamil Nadu.
- The new species has been named "Gymnothorax Tamilnaduensis" after Tamil Nadu and has been given the common name of "Tamil Nadu brown moray eel".
- A team of scientists from the Indian Council of Agriculture Research (ICAR) have discovered a new species of moray eel fish in the Cuddalore coast, which has been named Gymnothorax Tamilnaduensis or Tamil Nadu brown moray eel.

Defence News

Indian Army to Buy 310 Indigenous Advanced Towed Artillery Gun System

- The Ministry of Defence received a proposal from the Indian Army to buy 310 Advanced Towed Artillery Gun Systems (ATAGS) for deployment along the borders with China and Pakistan, marking a significant step towards 'Make-in-India' in the defense sector.
- The Indian Army has submitted a proposal worth more than USD 1 billion, which is currently being discussed.
- This would be the first order for the indigenous howitzer, which can strike targets at distances of up to 50 kilometers and is thought to be the best gun in its class.
- The forces have been testing the gun at various altitudes and terrain. They have been upgraded based on user suggestions.

IPS officer Rashmi Shukla named Director-General of SSB

- Senior Indian Police Service (IPS) officer, Rashmi Shukla has been appointed as the Director-General of the Sashastra Seema Bal (SSB). SSB is the border-guarding force deployed along Nepal and Bhutan border.
- Rashmi Shukla, a 1988 batch IPS officer of the Maharashtra cadre, was posted with the Central Reserve Police (CRPF).
- She was heading the State Intelligence Department in Maharashtra Police when the phones of Shiv Sena leader Sanjay Raut and Nationalist Congress Party leader Eknath Khadse were allegedly tapped in 2019.

IAF Participated in Exercise Shinyuu Maitri with Japan Air Self Defense Force

- The Indian Air Force (IAF) participated in Exercise Shinyuu Maitri with the Japan Air Self-Defence Force (JASDF).
- The Exercise Shinyuu Maitri is being organized on the sidelines of the Indo-Japan Joint Army Exercise, Dharma Guardian, which was conducted from 13 February 2023 to 02 March 2023 at Komatsu, Japan.
- The Indian Air Force is participating in Exercise Shinyuu Maitri 23 with one C-17 Globemaster III aircraft.
- The Exercise has been conducted on the 1st and 2nd of March 2023. The first phase of the exercise consists of discussions on transport operations and tactical maneuvering, followed by the second phase of flying drills by IAF's C-17 and JASDF C-2 transport aircraft.

INS Trikand participated in International Maritime Exercise 2023

- The Indian warship INS Trikand has arrived in Bahrain for her first participation in the International Maritime Exercise organised by the US-led Combined Maritime Forces, a 34-nation naval group.
- INS Trikand hosted Rear Adm Jean Michel Martinet of the French Navy, who is also the Vice Commander of IMX23 & Commander Task Force (East).
- INS Trikand crew also interacted with the planning team & ships from friendly Navies participating in the Exercise. The Captain of INS Trikand also called on Ambassador of India to Qatar, Piyush Srivastava.

FRINJEX-23 Indo-France Joint Military Exercise to commence at Thiruvananthapuram

- On March 7 and 8, 2023, the Indian Army and the French Army will hold their first joint military exercise, FRINJEX-23, at Pangode Military Station in Thiruvananthapuram, Kerala.
- The two armies are participating in this format for the first time, with each contingent consisting of a Company Group from the French 6th Light Armoured Brigade and Indian Army personnel stationed in Thiruvananthapuram.

In Ladakh, Colonel Geeta Rana is the first woman to command an army battalion

- Colonel Geeta Rana of the Corps of Electronics and Mechanical Engineers has taken over command of an independent field workshop in the Eastern Ladakh region with China after the Indian Army recently approved women officers for command posts.
- She is the first woman officer to do so. The Corps of Electronics and Mechanical Engineers' Colonel Geeta Rana is the first female officer to assume control of an Independent Field Workshop in a remote and forward area in Eastern Ladakh.

Indian Navy conducts major exercise TROPEX-23

- The Indian Navy's exercise, called the "Theatre Level Operational Readiness Exercise for 2023" (TROPEX-23), culminated in the Arabian Sea after running for four months from November 2022 to March 2023.
- TROPEX-23 witnessed the participation of approximately 70 Indian Navy ships, six submarines and over 75 aircraft.
- TROPEX is being is conducted in many phases to test Navy's transition from peacetime to hostilities.

- In the first phase, the Indian Navy had conducted coastal defence exercise 'Sea Vigil' along the entire coastline and Island territories of India on 12-13 January 2021.

Indian Navy gets first-ever privately made indigenized fuze of Anti-Submarine Warfare rocket

- In what is being seen as a major success for the "Make in India" initiative in defence sector, the Indian Navy has received a fully indigenised fuze for an anti-submarine warfare (ASW) underwater rocket, manufactured for the first time by a private Indian industry.
- This would be the first time the Indian Navy has placed a supply order for underwater ammunition fuzes with an Indian private sector industry.
- This marks the first time that the Indian Navy has procured an underwater ammunition fuze from an Indian private manufacturer. It is a major boost for the self-reliance of the Indian defence sector.

54th CISF Raising Day observed on March 10 across the country

- Every year on March 10, the Central Industrial Security Force (CISF) Raising Day is observed to mark the CISF's founding in 1969.
- The Ministry of Home Affairs' top-tier central armed police force, the CISF, is in charge of providing security protection for several public sector organisations, airports, seaports, power plants, and other significant infrastructure projects across the nation.
- This year, the 54th CISF Raising Day celebrated to appreciate the efforts and contributions of Central Industrial Security Force.

Army installed J&K's steep Doda district's tallest iconic national flag

- In the rugged Doda area of Jammu & Kashmir, the Army erected the tallest "Iconic National Banner".
- The highest tricolour in the Doda district, which has been erected on a 100-foot pole, was unfurled by Maj Gen Ajay Kumar, GOC Delta Force, Commander 9 Sector RR Brig. Samir K. Palande, DC Doda Vishesh Paul Mahajan, and SSP Abdul Qayoom.

Defence Ministry inks contract with HAL to procure 6 Dornier aircraft

- The defence ministry sealed a deal with Hindustan Aeronautics Limited (HAL) to procure six Dornier aircraft at a cost of Rs 667 crore for the Indian Air Force.
- The addition of the six aircraft will further bolster the operational capability of the IAF in remote areas, the defence ministry said announcing the contract.
- The aircraft was used by IAF for route transport roles and communication duties. Subsequently, it has also been used for training of transport pilots of the IAF.
- The aircraft is ideally suited for short-haul operations from semi-prepared and short runways of the North East and island chains of India.

India, France conduct Maritime Partnership Exercise (MPX)

- Indian Navy's indigenously built guided missile frigate, INS Sahyadri participat ed in a Maritime Partnership Exercise (MPX) with French Navy (FN) ships FS Dixmude, a Mistral Class Amphibious Assault Ship and FS La Fayette, a La Fayette Class Frigate, in the Arabian Sea. The partnership exercise was conducted on March 10-11.
- According to the Ministry of Defence, the exercise witnessed a wide spectrum of evolutions at sea which included cross-deck landings, boarding exercises and seamanship evolutions.

3rd edition of Exercise La Perouse- 2023 begins

- On March 13 and 14, 2023, the Indian Ocean Area will host the third edition of the multilateral exercise La Perouse.
- The Royal Australian Navy, French Navy, Indian Navy, Japanese Maritime Self Defence Force, Royal Navy, and United States Navy will all have people, ships, and essential helicopters participating in this event.
- Every two years exercise La Perouse, an exercise run by the French Navy, aims to improve maritime domain awareness and maritime cooperation among the participating navies in the Indo-Pacific region.

Joint India-Singapore exercise 'bold kurukshetra' concludes at Jodhpur

- Operation Bold Kurukshetra, a bilateral armour training exercise, was held from March 6–13, 2023, in Jodhpur Military Station in India.
- It was the 13th iteration, and the Singapore Army and Indian Army both took part. Both armies participated in the first command post exercise in the series, which included computer wargaming and planning components at the battalion and brigade levels.

- Participants in the exercise, which was held by the Indian Army, included members of the 42nd Battalion, Singapore Armoured Regiment, as well as an Indian Army Armoured Brigade.

Multi-lateral ASW Exercise Sea Dragon 23 commences

- The Indian Navy deployed a P8I aircraft to Guam, USA, on March 14, 2023, to participate in the third edition of 'Exercise Sea Dragon 23', a coordinated multilateral Anti-Submarine Warfare (ASW) exercise for Long Range MR ASW aircraft organized by the US Navy.
- The exercise, scheduled from March 15 to March 30, 2023, will focus on coordinated ASW tactics among the participating countries and will involve advanced ASW drills.

INS Dronacharya Receives Prestigious President Droupadi Murmu's Colour Award

- The Indian Navy's top gunnery school, INS Dronacharya, will be presented with the President's Colour in honor of its outstanding services.
- President Droupadi Murmu will be conferring the award as the highest recognition bestowed upon a unit by the President, who serves as the Supreme Commander of the armed forces, for its exceptional service to the country.

DRDO organises workshop on 'Human Factors Engineering in Military Platforms'

- A two-day workshop on "Human Factors Engineering in Military Platforms" was inaugurated by the Chief of Defence Staff General Anil Chauhan on March 15 in New Delhi.
- The workshop is being organized by the Defence Institute of Physiology and Al lied Sciences (DIPAS), which is a Delhi-based laboratory of the Defence Research and Development Organisation (DRDO).
- The objective of the workshop is to establish a policy framework and practices that ensure the scientific implementation of Human Factors Engineering (HFE) in the defence sector, thus contributing to the vision of 'Aatmanirbhar Bharat.'

Africa-India field training exercise AFINDEX-23 to be held in Pune

- The Africa-India Field Training Exercise (AFINDEX-2023) has begun with the participation of 100 participants from 23 African countries, including Botswana, Egypt, Ghana, Nigeria, Tanzania, and Zambia, among others.
- The exercise aims to improve interoperability and operational readiness for UN peacekeeping missions, and focuses on Humanitarian Mine Action and Peace Keeping Operations.
- The joint exercise is divided into four phases, including training of trainers, a Humanitarian Mine Action and Peace Keeping Operations Phase, and a validation exercise to assess the results of the training.
- The exercise seeks to enhance peace and security, exchange ideas, and promote a collaborative approach in capacity enhancement of African armies.
- Tactical drills, procedures, and the ability to operate jointly with seamless interoperability are the primary focus of the joint exercise.

Annual Bilateral Maritime Exercise Konkan 2023

- The annual bilateral maritime exercise called Konkan 2023 was conducted be tween the Indian Navy and the Royal Navy from 20th to 22nd March 2023 off the Konkan coast in the Arabian Sea.
- The Royal Navy is the United Kingdom's naval warfare force.
- The exercise involved INS Trishul, a guided missile frigate, and HMS Lancaster, a Type 23 guided missile frigate, and aimed to improve cooperation and learn best practices through various maritime drills.
- These drills covered air, surface, and sub-surface operations, such as gunnery shoots on an inflatable surface target called 'Killer Tomato,' helicopter operations, anti-aircraft, and anti-submarine warfare exercises, Visit Board Search and Seizure (VBSS), ship manoeuvres, and personnel exchange.
- The maritime exercise proved to be highly beneficial for the personnel of both navies, as it displayed a remarkable level of professionalism and enthusiasm throughout its execution.

GRSE launched the 'Most Silent Ship' INS Androth

- Garden Reach Shipbuilders and Engineers (GRSE), a shipbuilding company in India, has launched INS Androth, a vessel claimed to be the "most silent ship in the country" for the Indian Navy.
- The vessel is the first in a series of eight anti-submarine warfare shallow-watercraft to be delivered to the navy.

- The ships will be used for patrolling, search and rescue operations, and other military missions.
- The INS Androth has been designed to accommodate 50 crew members and is equipped with state-of-the-art communication systems, radars, and sonars to detect and track enemy submarines.

A Multi-Domain Exercise Vayu Prahar held at LAC

- Recently, during the on-going tensions between India and China at the Line of Actual Control (LAC), the Indian Army and Air Force carried out a 96-hour joint exercise named 'Vayu Prahar' in the eastern region.
- The exercise aimed to develop plans to achieve synergy in multi-domain operations by using air and land forces.
- It was conducted in the second week of March, and its primary objective was to enhance coordination between the Army and Air Force for effective operations in a multi-domain battlefield.

1st joint conference of army chiefs of India and African countries begins

- The inaugural joint conference between the Indian and African army chiefs is scheduled to take place in Pune, with Defense Minister Rajnath Singh as the guest of honor and Indian Army Chief General Manoj Pandey in attendance.
- This marks the first-ever conference of its kind between these nations, with 10 army chiefs and 31 representatives from African countries in attendance.
- Additionally, an exhibition under the Atmanirbhar Bharat initiative will be held to showcase defense products and target the African market.

India's Defence Exports to Reach Rs 40,000 Crore by 2026: Rajnath Singh

- India is set to become a major exporter of defense equipment and materials, with exports projected to be worth Rs 35,000 to Rs 40,000 crore by 2026.
- The announcement was made by Union minister Rajnath Singh during a speech at Symbiosis International University, where he emphasized the importance of self-reliance and creating an ecosystem that fosters self-confidence.
- Since adopting the Indianization program, India's defense exports have increased from Rs 900 crore in 2014 to Rs 15,000 crore to Rs 16,000 crore today.
- Singh expressed his pride in the country's defense forces, which are now meeting 80% of their needs through indigenous procurement.

First batch of Agniveers passes out of INS Chilka

- The "Agnipath" scheme is a defence recruitment initiative in India that aims to reduce the increasing salary and pension expenses by hiring short-term soldiers on a contract basis.
- These soldiers, known as 'Agniveer', will be initially recruited for four years, after which some of them may be retained.
- The scheme offers Indian youth an opportunity to serve in the Armed Forces and aims to achieve an optimal balance between youth and experience in the Army.
- Women will also be recruited into the armed forces under this scheme. Previously named "Tour of Duty", the initiative was launched in the presence of the Chiefs of the three Services.
- Currently, the Army recruits youth under Short Service Commission for an initial tenure of 10 years, which can be extended up to 14 years.

Banking News

RBI's new pilot project on coin vending machines

- Recently, RBI Governor Shaktikanta Das had stated during the most recent Monetary Policy Committee (MPC) address that the apex banking regulator, in collaboration with banks, would launch a pilot project to evaluate the operation of a QR-code based coin vending machine.
- The vending machines would dispense coins, with the appropriate amount debited from the customer's account via the United Payments Interface (UPI), instead of physically tendering banknotes.
- Customers would be able to withdraw coins in the desired quantities and denominations.
- The central concept here is to make coins more accessible.

HDFC Bank, IRCTC launch India's most rewarding co-branded travel credit card

- Indian Railway Catering and Tourism Corp Ltd (IRCTC) and HDFC Bank, announced the launch of a co-branded travel credit card. Known as the IRCTC HDFC Bank Credit Card, the newly launched co-branded card is available exclusively on NPCI's Rupay network.

- The card will provide exclusive benefits and maximum savings on bookings of train tickets booked through the IRCTC's ticketing website and through IRCTC Rail Connect app.
- The IRCTC HDFC Bank Credit Card will enable us to offer our card to millions of Indians across the country. Additionally, IRCTC HDFC Bank Credit card-holders will enjoy an attractive joining bonus, discounts on bookings and access to the several executive lounges at railway stations across the country.

SBI announces completion of $1 billion Syndicated Social Loan Facility

- The State Bank of India (SBI) announced the completion of a $1 billion syndicated social loan facility.
- It is the largest Environmental, Social, and Governance (ESG) loan by a commercial bank in the Asia Pacific and the second-largest social loan globally, the bank said.
- The facility of $1 billion was arranged through MLABs, MUFG bank and Taipei Fubon Commercial Bank Co. Ltd. MUFG and Taipei Fubon Commercial Bank are joint social loan coordinators while MUFG is the lead social loan coordinator for this transaction.

RBI Launches Two Surveys to Gather 'Useful Inputs' For Monetary Policy

- The Reserve Bank of India launched two key surveys, the results of which provide "useful inputs" for the central bank's by-monthly monetary policy. One of the surveys is to know inflation expectations of households and the other is to gauze the consumer confidence.
- The March 2023 round of Inflation Expectations Survey of Households (IESH), RBI said, aims at capturing subjective assessments on price movements and inflation, based on their individual consumption baskets, across 19 cities.
- Consumer confidence study too is conducted in 19 cities. The RBI said results of the surveys provide useful inputs for monetary policy. The next meeting of the RBI's rate setting panel Monetary Policy Committee is scheduled during April 6-8, 2023.

Kotak MF launches 'DigitALL' campaign to celebrate International Women's Day

- Kotak Mahindra Asset Management Company (Kotak Mutual Fund) has launched a digital campaign called 'DigitALL:

- Innovation and technology for gender equality', which calls for digital inclusion of all with the hashtag #IncludeAll.
- The digital campaign video showcases Kotak group's women employees sharing their stories about supporting and empowering other women in their lives by imparting them the knowledge of digital literacy.

PNB Signs MoU With Central Warehousing Corporation To Facilitate Finance To Farmers

- Punjab National Bank, nation's public sector bank and Central Warehousing Corporation have signed a Memorandum of Understanding to facilitate financing under e-NWR (Electronic Negotiable Warehousing Receipt).
- The partnership is aimed at providing easy access to finance to farmers/ food processors/ traders against the pledge of agriculture commodities stored in CWC warehouses.

RBI accords 'infra finance company' status to IREDA

- The Reserve Bank of India (RBI) granted an 'Infrastructure Finance Company (IFC)' status to Indian Renewable Energy Development Agency (IREDA) , a company statement said. It was earlier classified as an 'Investment and Credit Company (ICC)'.
- With the IFC status, IREDA will be able to take higher exposure in RE financing. The IFC status will also help the company to access a wider investor base for fund mobilisation, resulting in competitive rates for fundraising.

SBI raises Rs 3,717cr from its third AT1 bond sale

- State Bank of India (SBI) has raised Rs 3,717 crore through its third Basel III compliant Additional Tier 1 bond issuance in the current financial year at coupon rate of 8.25 per cent.
- SBI said the issue attracted overwhelming response from investors with bids of Rs 4,537 crore and was oversubscribed by about 2.27 times against the base issue of Rs 2,000 crore.
- The total number of bids were 53 indicating wider participation. The investors were across provident and pension funds and insurance companies.
- This issuance is also very significant as SBI has been able to successively diversify and raise long term Additional Tier 1 capital with a call option after 10 years and this will help the bank in managing its capital adequacy effectively.

Banks from 18 countries get RBI's nod to trade in rupee: Centre in RS

- The Reserve Bank of India (RBI) has permitted banks from 18 countries to open Special Vostro Rupee Accounts (SVRAs) to settle payments in rupees, the government said.
- Speaking in Rajya Sabha, Union Minister of State for Finance Bhagwat Kishanrao Karad said that 60 such approvals have been given by the RBI.
- These 18 nations include Botswana, Fiji, Germany, Guyana, Israel, Kenya, Malaysia, Mauritius, Myanmar, New Zealand, Oman, Russia, Seychelles, Singapore, Sri Lanka, Tanzania, Uganda and the United Kingdom.

RBI allows India and Tanzania to use national currencies for trading

- India and Tanzania have received approval from the Reserve Bank of India (RBI) to utilize their respective national currencies in bilateral trade settlements.
- This move is anticipated to decrease transaction costs and improve the effectiveness of cross-border trade, resulting in higher trade volumes and increased economic collaboration between the two nations.
- According to Binaya Pradhan, the Indian High Commissioner to Tanzania, the recent development of allowing the use of the Indian Rupee and the Tanzanian Shilling (Tsh) for settling bilateral trade is a positive development for the business community.

Canara Bank sells stake in Russian joint venture to SBI for Rs 121 crore

- Canara Bank has announced that it sold its stake in Commercial Indo Bank LLC (CIBL), a joint venture with State Bank of India (SBI), to SBI for approximately ₹121.29 crore.
- CIBL, which was established in 2003, operates in Russia and is owned 60% by SBI and 40% by Canara Bank.
- According to Canara Bank, the sale agreement was executed on November 11, 2022.
- According to a regulatory filing, Canara Bank has confirmed that it has received the full consideration amount of ₹121.29 crore for the sale of its stake in Commercial Indo Bank LLC to SBI.
- The agreement for the sale of Canara Bank's stake to SBI was announced in January of this year and the entire transfer of shares was completed on November 11, 2022, as per the agreement.

YES Bank issues first electronic bank guarantee with NeSL

- YES Bank has collaborated with National E-Governance Services Limited (NeSL) to issue its first electronic Bank Guarantee (e-BG).
- The integration of their digital document execution (DDE) platform has made it possible to completely digitize the previous paper-based process of issuing and maintaining Bank Guarantees.
- This includes the digital stamping and signing, which has significantly reduced the time it takes to issue Bank Guarantees.

First Citizens Bank Acquires Silicon Valley Bank

- First-Citizens Bank and Trust Company, based in Raleigh, North Carolina, has entered a purchase and assumption agreement with the Federal Deposit Insurance Corporation (FDIC) to acquire all loans and deposits of the recently failed Silicon Valley Bridge Bank in the United States.
- The FDIC established Silicon Valley Bridge Bank, National Association after the California Department of Financial Protection and Innovation closed down Silicon Valley Bank.

ICICI Lombard becomes first to offer 'Anywhere Cashless' feature

- ICICI Lombard General Insurance has introduced an industry-first feature for health insurance policyholders called 'Anywhere Cashless,' which allows them to receive cashless facilities at any hospital, regardless of whether or not it is currently part of ICICI Lombard's hospital network.
- However, the hospital must agree to accept the cashless facility for this feature to apply.

IDFC First Bank partners Crunchfish to demonstrate offline retail payments

- IDFC First Bank has announced its collaboration with the Swedish company Crunchfish to launch a pilot project to demonstrate offline retail payments.
- The bank is going to participate in the Reserve Bank of India's (RBI) pilot project that aims to enable offline payments.
- The project aims to provide digital payment services to customers and merchants even in areas without network connectivity.
- This project will provide support for offline retail payments based on a Digital Cash platform to the payment ecosystem of India.

- IDFC FIRST Bank will be one of the first few banks to be a part of this pilot project by HDFC Bank.

Axis Bank launches 'MicroPay' based on 'Pin on Mobile' technology for digital payments

- Axis Bank, one of India's top private sector banks, has introduced a ground-breaking payment solution called "MicroPay" in collaboration with technical partners Ezetap by Razorpay and MyPinpad.
- MicroPay is a "PIN on Mobile" solution that transforms a merchant's smartphone into a Point-of-Sale (POS) terminal, making digital payments easier and delivering a one-of-a-kind customer experience.

NPCI recommends PPI charges for UPI payments

- Starting from April 1, merchants carrying out transactions through the Unified Payments Interface (UPI) using Prepaid Payment Instruments (PPI) will be subjected to charges, according to a circular issued by the National Payments Corporation of India (NPCI).
- The National Payments Corporation of India (NPCI) has issued a circular stating that merchants conducting transactions on the Unified Payments Interface (UPI) using Prepaid Payment Instruments (PPI) will be charged an interchange fee of 1.1% on the transaction amount for amounts over Rs 2,000.

601st Meeting of Central Board of the Reserve Bank of India

- The central board of the Reserve Bank of India (RBI) chaired by Governor Shaktikanta Das, conducted its 601st meeting in Hyderabad to assess the current global and domestic economic conditions, along with the accompanying difficulties.
- According to a statement released by the RBI, during its meeting, the board evaluated the global and domestic economic scenario, as well as the associated obstacles, taking into account the influence of current global geopolitical events.

Summits and Conferences

PM Modi To Inaugurate 3-Day Raisina Dialogue in New Delhi

- The eighth edition of the annual Raisina Dialogue, the flagship conference on geopolitics and geo-strategy, begins in New Delhi. The annual Raisina Dialogue will be inaugurated by Prime Minister Narendra Modi.

- The Foreign Ministry is organizing the event in collaboration with the Observer Research Foundation from 2nd March to 4th March 2023.
- Italian Prime Minister Giorgia Meloni will be the chief guest and keynote speaker at its inaugural session.

Sarbananda Sonowal Inaugurated Global Conference & Expo on Traditional Medicine

- Union Minister of Ayush and Ports, Shipping & Waterways, Sarbananda Sonowal inaugurated the first B2B Global Conference & Expo on Traditional Medicine under Shanghai Cooperation Organisation (SCO) at Guwahati.
- The Union Minister informed that India has made the best use of available natural resources through Ayurveda and other traditional systems of medicine to provide healthcare to people as well as towards achieving the goal of Universal Health Coverage.
- The Global Center for Traditional Medicine of the World Health Organization (WHO-GCTM) being set up at Jamnagar with the support of India will help member countries to take enabling steps in their respective countries to strengthen education and practices of Traditional Medicine.

National Youth Parliament Festival Fourth Edition

- National Youth Parliament Festival Fourth Edition was held in the Parliament of India in thc national Capital, Ncw Dclhi.
- On the first day of the National Youth Parliament Festival (NYPF) finals in the Central Hall of Parliament, New Delhi, Minister of State for Youth and Sports Affairs Shri Nisith Pramanik gave a speech. During the first day, a continuation of the competitive session was planned.

President Murmu inaugurates 7th International Dharma Dhamma Conference

- President Droupadi Murmu inaugurated the 7th International Dharma Dhamma Conference 2023 in Bhopal, Madhya Pradesh. Over 15 countries will participate in the three-day conference.
- The 7th edition of the conference has a theme of "Eastern Humanism for the New Era" and has been planned in collaboration with Sanchi University of Buddhist-Indic Studies, whose vice chancellor Dr Neerja Gupta also joined President Murmu.

23rd Commonwealth Law Conference begins in Goa

- The 23rd Commonwealth Law Conference was inaugurated by Goa Governor P.S. Sreedharan Pillai.
- The five-day conference, which is being held from March 5-9, 2023, was also attended by Union Minister for Law and Justice Kiren Rijiju and Chief Minister of Goa Dr. Pramod Sawant.
- The Conference has 500 delegates from 52 countries in attendance.

Yoga Mahotsav 2023 marks the beginning of 100 Days Countdown of 9th International Yoga Day

- The celebration of Yoga Mahotsav 2023 marks the official beginning of the 100-day countdown to International Yoga Day 2023 and to sensitize and motivate the masses to participate in Yoga centric activities to widen the horizons of Yoga.
- The three-day Yoga Mahotsav 2023 is being held in the capital's Talkatora Stadium on 13-14 March and the Morarji Desai National Institute of Yoga (MDNIY) on 15 March.

India Hosts SCO International Conference on 'Shared Buddhist Heritage'

- With a focus on India's civilizational connections with the SCO states, the two-day international conference of the Shanghai Cooperation Organization (SCO) on "Shared Buddhist Heritage" was launched at Vigyan Bhawan in New Delhi.
- This historic gathering brings together Central Asian, East Asian, South Asian, and Arab nations to discuss "Shared Buddhist Heritage" and is the first of its kind.
- It takes place under India's leadership of the Shanghai Cooperation Organization (SCO) (from September 17, 2022, to September 23, 2023) for a year.

PM Modi inaugurated the Global Millets Conference

- Prime Minister Narendra Modi inaugurated the Global Millets (Shree Anna) Conference in New Delhi on 18th March, 2023.
- He will also address the gathering on the occasion.
- The conference will be attended by Agriculture Ministers of various countries, international scientists, nutritionists, health experts, start-up leaders and other stakeholders.

Sikkim hosts B20 meeting under India's G20 presidency

- The B20 Conference, held in Gangtok, Sikkim under India's G20 presidency, focused on exploring business opportunities in tourism, hospitality, pharmaceuticals, and organic farming.
- The event brought together delegations from 22 countries and over 100 Indian delegations to showcase Sikkim's potential in these sectors.
- This meeting will provide a unique opportunity to promote startups in North East India.
- The conference also presented an opportunity for India to address global challenges and showcase its leadership on the international stage.

PM Modi addressed 'One World TB Summit' at Varanasi

- During the One World TB Summit arranged by the Ministry of Health and Family Welfare (MoHFW) on World Tuberculosis Day, Prime Minister Narendra Modi highlighted India's powerful pharmaceutical industry as a significant advantage in the global battle against TB.
- He also mentioned that India has set a goal of eradicating TB by the year 2025.

India to host SCO-National Security Advisors meeting, Pakistan, China likely to join virtually

- The National Security Advisers of the Shanghai Cooperation Organisation (SCO) will convene in New Delhi, with China and Pakistan expected to attend virtually.
- Ajit Doval, the Indian National Security Adviser, will give the opening remarks, followed by discussions between SCO national security advisers and top officials.

Awards News

'Naatu Naatu' song from 'RRR' to be performed at the Oscars 2023 ceremony

- SS Rajamouli's 'RRR' movie, the popular song 'Naatu Naatu' which is nominated in the 'Best Original Song' category will be performed at the 95th Academy Awards or Oscar awards by singers Rahul Sipligunj and Kaala Bhairava in their Oscar debut.

- The song's music is composed by M.M. Keeravaani, while its lyrics are written by Chandrabose.

- The cross-cultural hit is nominated in the original song category alongside "This Is A Life" from "Everything Everywhere All at Once," "Applause" from "Tell It Like a Woman," and "Lift Me Up" from "Black Panther: Wakanda Forever," all of which are part of the scheduled performances for the 95th annual ceremony.

Sergio Pérez wins Saudi Arabia Grand Prix 2023

- At the Saudi Arabia Grand Prix of the 2023 Formula One season, Sergio Perez displayed a dominant performance and earned his first win.
- His teammate at Red Bull, Max Verstappen, secured the second position after starting from the 15th spot.
- Although Verstappen retained his lead in the championship standings with his fastest lap, Fernando Alonso was the focus of the battle for the final podium spot, finishing in third place.

Runner Lashinda Demus Awarded Olympic Gold Medal Over A Decade Later

- Lashinda Demus, a runner from the United States, has been awarded an Olympic gold medal at the age of 40, more than a decade after the 2012 London Games.
- This came after the International Olympic Committee stripped Natalya Antyukh, the original gold medalist in the 400-meter hurdles, of her title due to her involvement in the Russian doping scandal.
- Antyukh had beaten Demus by just 0.07 seconds on the London track, but historical evidence recovered from a Moscow testing laboratory database allowed the Athletics Integrity Unit to disqualify Antyukh's results from July 2012 through June 2013.

India Wins GSMA Government Leadership Award 2023

- Groupe Speciale Mobile Association (GSMA) has conferred Government Leadership Award 2023 to India for implementing best practices in telecom policy and regulation.
- GSMA, which represents more than 750 mobile operators and 400 companies in the telecom ecosystem, recognizes one country every year.

- India was declared winner in the ceremony held at Mobile World Congress Barcelona.

HDFC Bank's Sashidhar Jagdishan is 'BS Banker of the Year 2022'

- Sashidhar Jagdishan, managing director (MD) and chief executive officer (CEO) of HDFC Bank, has been chosen as the Business Standard Banker of the Year 2022.
- This award is given to him for his successful navigation of technology-related challenges while maintaining the bank's strong performance.
- The banking regulator had approved Jagdishan's appointment for a three-year period, after which he will be eligible for an extension. He will turn 58 this month. Jagdishan's journey in HDFC Bank started in 1996 as a manager in the finance function.

Union Health and Family Welfare Ministry gets Porter Prize 2023 in managing COVID-19

- Union Health and Family Welfare Ministry has received the Porter Prize 2023. It recognized the government's strategy in managing COVID-19, also the approach, and involvement of various stakeholders especially involvement of ASHA workers in the industry to create PPE Kits.
- The prize was announced during The India Dialog at Stanford University. The country's contribution in developing and manufacturing vaccines was also lauded.
- The theme of the two-day conference was The Indian Economy 2023: Innovation, Competitiveness and Social Progress.

Writer Vinod Kumar Shukla wins 2023 PEN/Nabokov Lifetime Achievement Award

- Vinod Kumar Shukla has won the PEN/Nabokov Award for Achievement in International Literature for lifetime achievement in literature, one of the most coveted literary prizes worldwide, after decades of composing acclaimed novels like

Naukar Ki Kameez (1979) and poetry collections like Sab Kuch Hona Bacha Rahega (1992).

- The award is conferred annually by PEN America.

Swachh Sujal Shakti Samman 2023 organized by the Ministry of Jal Shakti

- The "Swachh Sujal Shakti Samman 2023", organized by the Ministry of Jal Shakti to honour the women champions of rural water and sanitation sector, was graced by the President of India, Smt. Droupadi Murmu.
- This event organized in the run up to the International Women's Day, was to felicitate the exceptional and exemplary work being done at the grassroots level by women in the implementation of Swachh Bharat Mission – Grameen (SBM-G), Jal Jeevan Mission (JJM), Jal Shakti Abhiyan: Catch the Rain (JSA-CTR).
- 36 women WASH Champions were conferred with the 'Swachh Sujal Shakti Samman 2023' by the President of India and Union Minister of Jal Shakti.

BHEL wins CBIP Award 2022 for 'Best Contribution in Solar Energy'

- CBIP award 2022: Bharat Heavy Electricals Limited (BHEL) has been awarded the Central Board Of Irrigation And Power (CBIP) Award 2022 for 'Best Contribution in Solar Energy'.
- The award was received by Dr. Nalin Shinghal, CMD, BHEL, along with Ms. Renuka Gera, Director (IS&P), BHEL from Sh. R.K. Singh, Hon'ble Union Minister of Power and New & Renewable Energy, on CBIP Day. CBIP awards are conferred for outstanding contribution to the development of water, power and renewable energy sectors.

Mirabai Chanu won BBC Indian Sportswoman of The Year for 2022

- Tokyo Olympic Games silver-medallist weightlifter Mirabai Chanu has bagged the 2022 'BBC Indian Sportswoman of The Year' award after a public vote.
- The 28-year-old weightlifter from Manipur became the first athlete to win the award twice in a row after bagging it in 2021 as well.
- BBC Indian Sportswoman of the Year Award was launched in 2019 to celebrate sportswomen in India who have made their mark on the world stage.

Delhi International Airport among cleanest in Asia-Pacific, says ACI

- Delhi airport has been ranked among the cleanest airports in Asia-Pacific as a part of the Airport Council International (ACI)'s annual service quality award.
- The Indira Gandhi International Airport (IGIA), operated by DIAL, has bagged the award for Airport Service Quality (ASQ) best airport for 2022 in the category of over 40 Million Passengers Per Annum (MPPA).
- The airport service quality award is based on passenger surveys carried out to rate customer satisfaction on the day of travel.

Sir David Chipperfield Selected as the 2023 Laureate of the Pritzker Architecture Prize

- Civic architect, urban planner and activist, Sir David Alan Chipperfield has been selected as the 2023 Laureate of The Pritzker Architecture Prize, the award that is regarded internationally as architecture's highest honor.
- Chipperfield's storied career spans more than 40 years and includes 100-plus projects, ranging from civic, cultural, and academic buildings to residences and urban master planning throughout Asia, Europe, and North America.
- His built works, spanning over four decades, are expansive in typology and geography, including over one hundred works ranging from civic, cultural and academic buildings to residences and urban master planning throughout Asia, Europe and North America.

Union MoS Dr L. Murugan confers 8th National Photography Awards

- Union Minister of State for Information and Broadcasting Dr L. Murugan presented the 8th National Photography awards in New Delhi.
- A total of thirteen awards were presented during the ceremony today including 6 each in the Professional and Amateur category.
- The theme for the Professional category was "Life and Water", while in the Amateur category the theme was "Cultural Heritage of India".

Oscars 2023: RRR's "Naatu Naatu" wins Best Original Song

- Oscars awards 2023: The 95th Academy Awards (Oscars 2023) have announced that RRR's "Naatu Naatu" won Best Original Song.
- The song had to beat out songs like "Applause" from Tell It Like a Woman, "Hold My Hand" from Top Gun: Maverick, "Lift Me Up" from Black Panther: Wakanda Forever, and "This is Life" from Everything Everywhere All at Once.
- The Oscars 2023 was accepted by lyricist Chandrabose and composer Keeravani.

India received Golden & Silver Star at 'Golden City Gate Tourism Awards

- The International Golden City Gate Tourism Awards 2023 in the categories of "TV/Cinema Commercials International and Country International" were won by the Indian Ministry of Tourism and Government of India, respectively.
- As part of a global effort on advertising in the post-Covid period to reopen opportunities in India, the award has been granted to promotional films/television ads made by the Ministry.
- On March 8, 2023, at ITB, Berlin, Shri Arvind Singh, Secretary (Tourism), Government of India, accepted the honours.

Oscars 2023: The Elephant Whisperers wins in Best Documentary Short Category

- The Elephant Whisperers, a Netflix documentary short from Kartiki Gonsalves and Guneet Monga, has won the 95th Academy Awards' Best Documentary Short award.
- The movie was up against 'Stranger At The Gate', 'Haulout', and 'How Do You Measure a Year?' The award is an honour of "my motherland, India," said director Gonzalves.

Oscars awards 2023: Check the complete list of winners

- The 95th Academy Awards (Oscars Awards 2023) are finally announced and the fans are excited to know how India fares at Oscars Awards 2023.
- The Academy Awards, or Oscars Awards 2023, which were originally held in 1929, recently celebrated their 95th anniversary.

- The Oscars Awards 2023 held on March 13 IST in Los Angeles' Dolby theatre. It was hosted by popular late night show host Jimmy Kimmel.
- Check the complete list here.

Vyas Samman 2022: Gyan Chaturvedi to be awarded for 'Pagalkhana'

- Vyas Samman 2022: Pagalkhana, a 2018 satirical novel by renowned Hindi author Dr. Gyan Chaturvedi, has been chosen for the 32nd Vyas Samman.
- Dr. Chaturvedi's Pagalkhana (mental hospital) was chosen for the prestigious Vyas Samman by a selection committee led by distinguished author Prof. Ramji Tiwari.
- The KK Birla Foundation founded the annual Vyas Samman in 1991, which is awarded to a superb piece of Hindi literature authored by an Indian citizen and published within the previous ten years. A 4 lakh rupee award is offered.

RBI Governor Shaktikanta Das Named 'Governor of the Year' by Central Banking

- Shaktikanta Das, Governor of the Reserve Bank of India, has been honored with the title "Governor of the Year" for 2023 by Central Banking, an international economic research journal.
- The publication praised Das for his steady leadership during challenging periods, including the collapse of a significant non-banking company, the initial and second waves of the COVID-19 pandemic, and inflationary pressures due to Russia's invasion of Ukraine.
- This is the second time an Indian central bank governor has received the award, with Raghuram Rajan being the previous recipient in 2015.

Sivasankari, the Renowned Tamil Writer, Honored with Saraswati Samman 2022

- The KK Birla Foundation has announced that Tamil writer Sivasankari will be the recipient of the prestigious Saraswati Samman award for the year 2022, for her 2019 memoir, Surya Vamsam.

- This award is one of the most esteemed recognitions in Indian literature, and comes with a cash prize of Rs 15 lakh, a plaque, and a citation.

- Sivasankari is a prolific writer with a career spanning over 50 years, during which she has written 36 novels, 48 novellas, 150 short stories, 15 travelogues, seven collections of essays, and three biographies, including one on former Indian Prime Minister Indira Gandhi.

- Her literary contributions have been widely recognized, and her works have been translated into several Indian languages, as well as English, Japanese, and Ukrainian.

Indian American to receive National Humanities medal from Joe Biden

- The White House has announced that US President Joe Biden will bestow the 2021 National Humanities Medals upon several recipients, including Indian-American actress, comedian, and writer Mindy Kaling, also known as Vera Mindy Chokalingam.

- The National Medal of Arts is the most prestigious award granted by the US government to artists, arts advocates, and organizations.

Nepali cricketer Asif Sheikh wins 2022 Christopher Martin-Jenkins Spirit of Cricket Award

- Aasif Sheikh, a wicketkeeper from Nepal, has been awarded the 2022 Christopher Martin-Jenkins Spirit of Cricket Award for his act of sportsmanship during a T20 international match.

- He refused to run out Ireland's Andy McBrine, who was accidentally tripped over by Kamal Airee, the bowler. Judges also highly commended England's Jos Buttler and Ben Stokes.

- In 2013, the Marylebone Cricket Club (MCC) and the BBC established the Spirit of Cricket Award to honor the memory of Christopher Martin-Jenkins, a former MCC president and BBC Test Match Special commentator who was dedicated to promoting the values of the sport.

Bombay Jayashri chosen for Sangita Kalanidhi Award 2023 by Music Academy

- The Music Academy has announced that the Sangita Kalanidhi award for 2023 will be presented to Bombay Jayashri, a Padma Shri awardee and renowned Carnatic vocalist.
- According to the Academy's press release, Jayashri is considered as one of the leading Carnatic musicians of the present time.
- She received her initial training in Carnatic music from her parents and later studied under TR Balamani and Lalgudi G Jayaraman, a celebrated violin maestro.
- In addition to Carnatic music, Jayashri has also received training in Hindustani music, classical dance, and the veena.

Luis Caffarelli won the 2023 Abel Prize

- Luis Caffarelli, 74, has won the 2023 Abel Prize "for his seminal contributions to regularity theory for nonlinear partial differential equations including free-boundary problems and the Monge-Ampère equation".
- The prize includes a monetary award of 7.5 million kroner (roughly $ 720,000) and a glass plaque designed by Norwegian artist Henrik Haugan.
- It is awarded by The Norwegian Academy of Science and Letters, on behalf of the Ministry of Education.

M T Vasudevan Nair awarded Kerala's highest civilian honour

- The highest civilian honor in Kerala, the "Kerala Jyothi," was awarded to the writer M T Vasudevan Nair.
- The second-highest award, "Kerala Prabha," was shared by actor Mammootty, former civil service officer T Madhava Menon, and writer Omchery NN Pillai.

- Arif Muhammad Khan, the Governor of Kerala, has presented the inaugural edition of the "Kerala Puraskarngal" awards, which recognize individuals who have made notable contributions to various aspects of social life.
- The awards were presented in three categories – "Kerala Jyothi," "Kerala Prabha," and "Kerala Shri."

NGO from Assam honoured with Children's Champion Award

- Tapoban, an NGO based in Pathsala, Assam, which focuses on supporting children with special needs and autism, has been honored with the prestigious Children's Champion Award 2023 in the health and nutrition category.
- This award is presented by the Delhi Commission for Protection of Child Rights and acknowledges individuals and organizations that have made significant contributions to the welfare of children in various areas such as education, justice, health, nutrition, sports, and creative arts.

Kashmir's Aliya Mir honoured with Wildlife Conservation Award 2023

- The Union Territory has awarded wildlife conservationist Aliya Mir for her exceptional efforts in conservation.
- Aliya is the first woman from Jammu and Kashmir to work for Wildlife SOS and is the first woman in the region to receive this honour.
- She received the award from Lt. Manoj Sinha at the World Forestry Day celebrations hosted by the Jammu and Kashmir Collective Forests.
- Aliya was recognized for her remarkable contributions to wildlife conservation, including rescuing and releasing wild animals, caring for injured animals, and saving bears in Kashmir.

Bangabandhu Sheikh Mujibur Rahman honoured with literary award

- The Foundation of SAARC Writers and Literature (FOSWAL) presented a unique literary award to Bangabandhu Sheikh Mujibur Rahman of Bangladesh for his trilogy of books, which includes The Unfinished Memoirs, The Prison Diaries, and the New China 1952.

- FOSWAL acknowledged Bangabandhu Sheikh Mujibur Rahman's exceptional literary skills and awarded him for his outstanding literary excellence in the trilogy, according to the citation provided by the organization.

Kerala Sangeetha Nataka Academy awards declared

- The Kerala Sangeetha Nataka Akademi has announced the fellowships, awards, and Gurupuja Puraskaram of the year 2022.
- Theatre person Gopinath Kozhikode, music director P.S. Vidyadharan, and Chenda/Edakka artist Kalamandalam Unnikrishnan have been selected for the Kerala Sangeetha Nataka Akademi fellowships for their contribution to the respective fields.

Naveen Jindal honoured with 'Lifetime Achievement Award' by University of Texas

- Naveen Jindal has been awarded a lifetime achievement award by the University of Texas at Dallas for his accomplishments in industry, politics, and education.
- Jindal, who graduated from the University in 1992, received the award in a ceremony.
- This award is the highest recognition given to an alumnus by the University of Texas, Dallas and is presented to those whose contributions have positively impacted society.
- Aziz Sancar, a Nobel Laureate, was the first person to receive the Lifetime Achievement Award from the University of Texas at Dallas.

Agreements News

Godrej & Boyce, Renmakch sign MoU to develop a 'Make-in-India' value chain for Indian Railways

- Godrej & Boyce, the flagship company of the Godrej Group, announced that its business Godrej Tooling has partnered with Renmakch, to collaborate on Machinery & Plant (M&P) projects for Railways and Metro Rail, offering world-class equipment that is 'Made in India'.
- With this alliance, Godrej & Boyce will now be able to offer a complete value chain ranging from design to build for the Railways and also bid on larger projects. The Company has been a trusted partner of the Indian Railways for over 15 years.

Paralympic Committee of India signs MoU with Makers Hive and Vilay Sports

- Makers Hive and Vilay Sports have signed a Memorandum of Understanding (MOU) with the Paralympic Committee of India (PCI), which was witnessed by Dr Deepa Malik, the current president of PCI, para-athlete Shri Devendra Jhajharia, and others.
- The MOU signing marks a significant collaboration between the three organizations.
- Vilay Sports is a sports management company that aims to establish and maintain partnerships across various sports domains.

Tata Steel Mining signs MoU with GAIL to get clean fuel

- In order to reduce carbon footprint in its operations, Tata Steel Mining Limited has signed a memorandum of understanding with GAIL (India) Limited for supply of natural gas to its ferro alloys plant at Athgarh in Odisha's Cuttack district.
- According to the MoU, GAIL will supply the agreed quantity of natural gas through its pipeline from Gujarat to Athgarh.

India and Australia sign a framework mechanism for mutual recognition of qualifications

- India and Australia signed a Framework Mechanism for Mutual Recognition of Qualifications that will help ease the mobility of students and professionals between the two countries.
- While the two countries will recognise the degrees, professional registrations of engineering, medicine and law pass-outs will remain outside the framework's ambit.

RBI, Central Bank of UAE sign MoU to promote innovation in financial products and services

- The Reserve Bank of India (RBI) on March 15 said that it has signed a Memorandum of Understanding (MoU) with the Central Bank of United Arab Emirates for promoting innovation in financial product and services.
- Both central banks will collaborate on various emerging areas of FinTech, especially Central Bank Digital Currencies (CBDCs), and explore interoperability between the CBDCs of UAE's central bank and the RBI.
- Central Bank of UAE and RBI will jointly conduct proof-of-concept (PoC) and pilot(s) of bilateral CBDC bridge to facilitate cross-border CBDC transactions of remittances and trade.

Defence Ministry inks deal worth over Rs 1,700 crore to boost critical weapon system production

- The Ministry of Defence (MoD) signed a contract worth over Rs 1,700 crore with BrahMos Aerospace Private Limited (BAPL) for the procurement of Next Generation Maritime Mobile Coastal Batteries (Long range) (NGMMCB-LR) and BrahMos Missiles under the Buy (Indian) Category.
- Delivery of NGMMCBs equipped with supersonic BrahMos Missiles is expected to start in 2027, and they will significantly improve the Indian Navy's ability to carry out multi-directional maritime strikes.

NADA and NCERT sign MoU to strengthen value-based sports education amongst school children and teachers

- The National Anti-Doping Agency (NADA) under the Youth Affairs and Sports Ministry; and the National Council of Educational Research and Training (NCERT) signed an MoU to strengthen value-based sports education amongst school children and teachers.
- The key activities that will be undertaken through this MoU include developing e-content in an accessible format on sports values and ethics. The UNESCO Value-Based Sports Education toolkit will also be promoted in every classroom under the MoU.
- This MoU will amplify NADA's outreach efforts multi-fold, in collaboration with NCERT. She stressed that the MoU will also help in creating awareness at the grassroots.

Defence Ministry Inks Rs 3700 Cr Contracts with BEL for Radars and Receivers

- The Indian Defence Ministry has recently signed two contracts with Bharat Electronics Limited (BEL) worth more than Rs 3,700 crore, with the aim to enhance the operational capabilities of the Indian Air Force.
- Under the Buy Indian – IDMM (Indigenously Designed Developed and Manufactured) category, both projects are part of the ongoing vision of Aatmanirbhar Bharat.
- The first contract, worth over Rs 2,800 crore, involves the supply of Medium Power Radars (MPR) 'Arudhra', which have been designed and developed by the Defence Research and Development Organisation (DRDO) and will be manufactured by BEL.
- The second contract, with a cost of approximately Rs 950 crore, relates to Radar Warning Receivers (RWR).

World Bank commits $1 billion to India for public healthcare infra

- The Centre and the World Bank have signed two complementary loans of $500 million each to support and enhance the country's health sector development.
- Through this combined financing of $1 billion, the World Bank will support India's flagship Pradhan Mantri-Ayushman Bharat Health Infrastructure Mission (PM-ABHIM), launched in October 2021.
- The agreement was signed by Rajat Kumar Mishra, Additional Secretary, Department of Economic Affairs, Ministry of Finance on behalf of the Government of India and Auguste Tano Kouamé, Country Director, India, World Bank.
- Both the loans are from the International Bank for Reconstruction and Development (IBRD), having a final maturity of 18.5 years, including a grace period of 5 years.

HCL Technologies partners Microsoft to bring quantum computing to clients

- Domestic information technology (IT) services firm, HCL Technologies, announced a partnership with Azure Quantum, Microsoft's quantum cloud computing service.
- Through this partnership, HCLTech will offer cloud-based quantum computing services to businesses using Microsoft's platform as a technology stack.

- The services will be provided through HCLtech's Q-Labs, which is already one of Microsoft's partners offering Azure Quantum Credit.

India, US to sign memorandum of understanding on semiconductors

- The United States and India will sign a memorandum of understanding on semiconductors as both countries discuss coordination of investment and continue dialogue around policies to spur private investment, U.S. Commerce Secretary Gina Raimondo said.
- The dialogue comes close on the heels of the launch of the inauguration of the initiative on Critical and Emerging Technology (iCET).
- Raimondo, who is on a four-day trip to India, is accompanied by the chief executive officers of 10 U.S. companies and is scheduled to meet India's trade minister.
- The two nations will map the semiconductor supply chain together and identify opportunities for joint ventures and technology partnerships, Raimondo added.

Australia, India agree on strengthening economic, defence ties

- Australia and India have agreed to accelerate a broader economic partnership and to boost their defence ties, Australian Prime Minister Anthony Albanese said in New Delhi.
- Last year the two countries signed a free trade deal called the Economic Cooperation and Trade Agreement (ECTA), the first signed by India with a developed country in a decade.
- However, a much larger Comprehensive Economic Cooperation Agreement (CECA) has been stuck in negotiations for over a decade.

India & World Bank signs loan agreement for construction of Green National Highway Corridors Project in 4 States

- The Government of India and the World Bank have signed an agreement for the Green National Highway Corridors Project, with loan assistance of $500 million against total project cost of $1,288.24 million (Rs 7,662.47 crore).
- An aggregate length of 781 km will be constructed in the states of Himachal Pradesh, Rajasthan, Uttar Pradesh and Andhra Pradesh.

Government signs MoU with 27 steel companies, kickstarting Rs 6,322-crore PLI scheme

- The Ministry of Steel has signed 57 Memorandums of Understanding (MoUs) with 27 companies for specialty steel production under the Production Linked Incentive (PLI) Scheme.
- The government has allocated Rs. 6322 crores to boost the steel sector and generate an investment of about Rs. 30,000 crores, creating an additional capacity of approximately 25 million tonnes of specialty steel over the next five years.
- This move is expected to create numerous direct and indirect job opportunities while helping India achieve its goal of becoming the world's third-largest economy by 2030-31.

Schemes News

Select central govt employees get one-time option to opt for old pension scheme

- In a major move, a select group of central government employees have been given a one-time option to opt for old pension scheme, according to a Personnel Ministry order. The employees who joined the central government services against posts advertised or notified before December 22, 2003, the day National Pension System (NPS)
- was notified, are eligible to join the old pension scheme under the Central Civil Services (Pension) Rules, 1972 (now 2021), said the order.
- This option may be exercised by the government servants concerned latest by August 31, 2023. The move came following various representations/references and court decisions in this regard, it said.

'SWAYATT' promoting start-ups on GeM, turning to be a huge success

- The government e-Marketplace (GeM) held a celebration to celebrate "SWAYATT," a programme to support start-ups, women, and youth advantage through e-Transactions on GeM, which has been a major success. SWAYATT is a programme that seeks to increase the benefits of e-Transactions on government e-Marketplaces (GeM) for startups, women, and young people.
- It is important to note that by registering more than 8.5 lakh Micro and Small Businesses (MSEs) on the GeM portal and helping MSEs secure over Rs. 1.87 lakh crore in sales spread across 68 lakh+ orders, the GeM promotes social and financial inclusion.

Ministry of Culture administers 'Financial Assistance to Veteran Artists' scheme

- The Ministry of Culture administers a Scheme by the name of 'Financial Assistance for Veteran Artists' (erstwhile 'Scheme for Pension and Medical Aid to Artistes') to provide financial assistance to veteran artists of the country of the age of 60 years and above in the form of monthly artists' pension.
- However, the disbursement of financial assistance to the recommended artists is subject to submission of requisite documents by the beneficiaries selected under the Scheme such as Digital Life Certificate, Income Certificates etc.
- Ministry of Culture has entrusted the Life Insurance Corporation (LIC) vide an MoU in 2009 for disbursing the monthly artists pension to selected beneficiaries prior to the year 2017.

Govt aims to strengthen MSME sector with Competitive (LEAN) Scheme

- To encourage micro, small, and medium-sized enterprises (MSMEs) to adopt particular manufacturing practices, the Indian central government introduced a revamped version of the MSME Competitive (LEAN) Programme.
- The programme, which was initially launched under the MSME Champions Program, will help Indian MSMEs by boosting their quality, productivity, and performance.
- Through the programme, MSMEs will work with professional LEAN consultants to complete the basic, intermediate, and advanced levels of the LEAN Scheme by using LEAN manufacturing technologies including 5S, Kaizen, KANBAN, the visual workspace, and Poka Yoka.

What is Research, Education and Training Outreach (REACHOUT) scheme?

- The Research, Education and Training Outreach (REACHOUT) scheme is a program launched by the Indian government to promote research, education and training in the country.
- The Indian Ministry of Earth Sciences has initiated the REACHOUT Scheme to advance research, education, and training in the realm of Earth Sciences.
- The program aims to encourage collaboration between academic institutions, industry, and government to improve the quality of education and research in India.

Short Stories collection "The Book of Bihari Literature" by Abhay K

- Bihar Minister of Industry, Samir Kumar Mahaseth has released a book titled "The Book of Bihari Literature", edited by Abhay Kumar, an Indian poet- diplomat, during Grand Trunk Road Initiatives 3.0(GTRi 3.0) held in Patna, Bihar.
- The book, published by HarperCollins, is a collection of short stories and poems written over a period of 2600 years, translated into English from various languages such as Angika, Bajjika, Bhojpuri, Magahi, Maithili, Hindi, Urdu, Pali, Sanskrit, and Farsi.
- Samir Kumar Mahaseth insisted that the book is an important contribution towards promoting the rich literature of Bihar across India and the world.

Anurag Behar authors the New Book "A Matter of the Heart: Education in India"

- Anurag Behar, the CEO of Azim Premji Foundation and founding vice-chancellor of Azim Premji University, has authored a new travel book titled "A Matter of the Heart: Education in India".
- The book is a collection of 110 stories, based on Behar's experiences working at the foundation, and sheds light on the state of education in India beyond the major cities.
- Through his writing, Behar pays tribute to the educators who are shaping the future of the country.
- The book has been published by Westland Nonfiction, which is a division of Nasadiya Technologies Pvt Ltd.
- Behar is a well-known educationist and leader in India's social sector.

Shrimant Kokate's 1st book in English "Chhatrapati Shivaji Maharaj" released

- Shrimant Kokate, a well-known Marathi author and historian, has recently released his first English book titled "Chhatrapati Shivaji Maharaj (illustrated)", which has been translated by Dilip Chavan.
- The book was released by Amol Kolhe, a popular MP and actor known for his portrayals of Chhatrapati Shivaji Maharaj and Sambhaji Maharaj in Marathi TV series.
- Kokate is renowned for his four books on Shivaji, which have received great reviews and have been widely read.

Ghulam Nabi Azad's Autobiography 'Azaad' released soon

- Ghulam Nabi Azad, a former Chief Minister of Jammu and Kashmir and Union Minister, has written an honest and forthright autobiography, which will be launched in New Delhi on April 5.

A book titled 'Basu Chatterji: And Middle-of-the-Road Cinema' released

- A new book titled 'Basu Chatterji: And Middle-of-the-Road Cinema' has been released, which chronicles the life and times of the veteran Indian filmmaker Basu Chatterjee.
- The book is written by Aniruddha Bhattacharjee, an award-winning author, and has been published by Penguin Random House India (PRHI).
- The book takes readers behind the scenes of some of Chatterjee's most memorable films, such as 'Chitchor', 'Sara Aakash', 'Khatta Meetha' and 'Baton Baton Mein'.
- It provides insights into Chatterjee's filmmaking style and the cultural and social context in which his films were made.

Tamil writer Perumal Murugan's novel 'Pyre' makes it to International Booker 2023 longlist

- Perumal Murugan's novel 'Pyre', which deals with caste-based discrimination, has been nominated for the 2023 International Booker Prize longlist.
- Originally written in Tamil under the title 'Pukkuli', the book follows the story of a couple from different castes who flee their village, triggering a dark and om inous tale.
- The book was translated into English by Aniruddhan Vasudevan in 2016.

A book titled "Phoolange" penned by Darjeeling-based writer Lekhnath Chhetri

- Penguin Random House India (PRHI) has announced that the English translation of the Nepali novel "Phoolange" will be released on April 17th.
- The book is written by Lekhnath Chhetri, a writer based in Darjeeling, and focuses on the failed Gorkha movement for a separate state.
- The original Nepali version of the novel was shortlisted for the Madan Puraskar, which is Nepal's most prestigious literary award, in 2021.

A book titled "War & Women" written by Dr MA Hasan released

- During the 52nd Session of the United Nations Human Rights Council (UNHRC) in Geneva, Switzerland, a book entitled "War and Women" was launched.
- The author, Dr M A Hasan, presented the book, which highlights the suffering of Bengali women who were victims of sexual violence perpetrated by the Pakistan Army during the 1971 war.
- The event was organized by the Bangladesh Freedom Fighters Sansad in Europe, and it was considered a significant moment for raising awareness about the issue.

Niyogi Books released a new book 'Why can't Elephants be Red?'

- Vani Tripathi Tikoo, an actor and member of the Indian censor board, has written her debut children's book titled "Why Can't Elephants be Red??" published by Niyogi Books.
- The book is about a two-and-a-half-year-old girl named Akku who is imaginative, adventurous, and growing up in Gurgaon and Singapore.

Anurag Behar authors the New Book "A Matter of the Heart: Education in India"

- Anurag Behar, the CEO of Azim Premji Foundation and founding vice-chancellor of Azim Premji University, has authored a new travel book titled "A Matter of the Heart: Education in India".
- The book is a collection of 110 stories, based on Behar's experiences working at the foundation, and sheds light on the state of education in India beyond the major cities.
- Through his writing, Behar pays tribute to the educators who are shaping the future of the country.
- The book has been published by Westland Nonfiction, which is a division of Nasadiya Technologies Pvt Ltd.
- Behar is a well-known educationist and leader in India's social sector.

Business News

Foxconn to invest nearly 1 billion USD in Bengaluru

- A 300-acre plot adjacent to Bengaluru's international airport has been agreed upon by Foxconn, a Taiwanese company that assembles iPhones, as the location for its largest technology manufacturing campus in India.
- The Foxconn company plans to make incremental investments totaling less than $1 billion, helping the southern state establish itself as a hub for electronic manufacturing and positioning itself as a rival to China for suppliers.

RBI imposes restrictions on Musiri Urban Co-operative Bank

- The Reserve Bank of India imposed a Rs 5,000 cap on withdrawals by individual customers from Tamil Nadu-based Musiri Urban Co-operative Bank as part of several restrictions slapped on the lender due to its deteriorating financial condition.
- The restrictions on the lender will remain in force for six months from the close of business on March 3 and are subject to review, the RBI said in a statement.
- With curbs in place, the cooperative bank, without approval of the RBI, cannot grant loans, make any investment, and disburse any payment. The lender cannot also dispose of any of its properties, among others.

PMLA, 2002 Amended to Include Cryptocurrency Trade

- Finance Ministry has tweaked the anti-money laundering law by bringing cryptocurrencies and other virtual digital assets trade under its ambit.
- This means that exchanges, custodians, and wallet providers, among others in crypto-related trade, will fall under the Prevention of Money Laundering Act.
- The government has imposed money laundering provisions on cryptocurrencies or virtual assets as it looks to tighten oversight of digital assets.

Pfizer will spend $43 billion to acquire Seagen

- Pfizer is spending about $43 billion to acquire Seagen to reach deeper into new cancer treatments that target tumor cells while sparing surrounding healthy tissue.
- The pharmaceutical giant said it will pay $229 in cash for each share of Seagen Inc. Pfizer then plans to let the biotech drug developer "continue innovating," except with more resources than it would have alone, Pfizer Chairman and CEO Albert Bourla told.

IDFC Mutual Fund (MF) has rebranded itself as Bandhan Mutual Fund

- IDFC Mutual Fund has rebranded itself as Bandhan Mutual Fund. The change in name will be effective from March 13. All the schemes of the fund house will be renamed to replace the word 'IDFC' with the word 'Bandhan'.
- The rebranding includes a change of the name and the logo. According to the fund house, the name and ownership change will have no bearing on the investment strategy and processes of the schemes.
- The Securities and Exchange Board of India had cleared the Bandhan-linked consortium's proposed acquisition of IDFC Mutual Fund in December 2022.

Microsoft inks licensing deal with cloud gaming provider Boosteroid

- Microsoft strikes a deal to make Xbox PC video games available on the Boosteroid cloud gaming platform, its latest move to appease antitrust regulators scrutinising its purchase of game maker Activision Blizzard.
- The US tech giant said the 10-year agreement would also include Activision Blizzard titles like the popular Call of Duty franchise if or when the acquisition gets approved.
- Microsoft aims to boost its firepower in the booming videogaming market against leaders Tencent and Sony, and lay the base for its investment in metaverse.

BIS Launches 'Learning Science via Standards' Initiative to Benefit Students

- The Bureau of Indian Standards (BIS) has launched the "Learning Science via Standards" initiative to promote science learning among school students.
- This program aims to improve students' learning outcomes in science and promote an interest in science education by providing them with access to national and international standards related to science.
- The initiative is part of BIS's efforts to improve the quality of education in India and support the government's efforts to make India a global leader in science and technology.

UBS agrees to buy crisis-hit Credit Suisse for $3.2 billion in historic deal

- To prevent further turmoil in the global banking system, Swiss authorities have orchestrated a shotgun merger between UBS and Credit Suisse, with UBS agreeing to buy its rival for 3 billion Swiss francs ($3.23 billion) and assuming up to $5.4 billion in losses.

- The regulators' intervention was prompted by concerns that a crisis of confidence in Credit Suisse could have a widespread impact on the financial system.
- The deal is expected to be completed by the end of 2023.

Ashneer Grover launched cricket fantasy sports app 'CrickPe'

- Ashneer Grover, co-founder of BharatPe, has launched a new cricket-focused fantasy sports app named CrickPe ahead of the Indian Premier League (IPL) tournament.
- This app will compete against rivals such as Dream11, Mobile Premier League (MPL), and Games24x7's My11Circle.
- Third Unicorn Pvt Ltd, founded by Ashneer Grover, has raised $4 million in seed funding from more than two dozen angel investors, including Anmol Singh Jaggi, Anirudh Kedia, and Vishal Kedia.
- Previously, Grover was associated with BharatPe and Grofers, both of which are unicorns.
- The app is targeting the upcoming IPL tournament for its launch and is allowing users to participate in contests for IPL matches starting from March 31, 2023.

BCCI Announces Herbalife as its Official Partner for TATA IPL 2023

- Herbalife, a leading global nutrition company, has teamed up with the Board of Control for Cricket in India (BCCI) to become an official partner of the TATA Indian Premier League (IPL) for the 2023 season.
- This partnership brings together two strong brands that share a passion for sports.
- The IPL is a beloved cricket tournament for fans in India and around the world, while Herbalife is known for providing high-quality, science-based nutrition products that help athletes perform at their best.
- The TATA IPL 2023 is set to take place in India from March 31 to May 28, 2023.

Obituaries News

Former Chief Justice of India AM Ahmadi passes away at 90

- Former Chief Justice of India A.M. Ahmadi has passed away at the age of 90. Ahmadi was the chief justice from 1994 to 1997.

- His judicial career as a City Civil and Session Court judge in Ahmedabad, he was the only Chief Justice of India who started at the very lowest rank to rise to the highest position of the Indian judiciary.

Veteran actor-director Satish Kaushik passes away at 67

- Veteran actor-writer-director Satish Kaushik has passed away at the age of 67.
- He was born on April 13, 1965, in Haryana, Kaushik was an alumnus of the NSD and the FTII, and started his film career in the early 1980s.
- He was an Indian actor, comedian, screenwriter, director and producer. He acted in theatres before finding his break in Bollywood

Actor Sameer Khakhar who played role of Khopdi in 'Nukkad' passes away

- Sameer Khakhar, an experienced actor who had worked in theater, television, and movies, has passed away. He is most remembered for his portrayal of the character "Khopdi" in the popular TV series "Nukkad."
- Sameer Khakhar's career spanned across various genres of entertainment, but his performance as Khopdi was particularly notable, earning him recognition and praise from audiences.
- His death is a loss to the industry and those who appreciated his talents as a versatile performer.

Director Pradeep Sarkar passes away at 67

- Pradeep Sarkar, a renowned filmmaker who directed successful movies like Parineeta and Mardaani, has passed away at the age of 67.
- He began his career in directing with the film Parineeta in 2005, starring Vidya Balan, and went on to direct other popular movies such as Laga Chunari Mein Daag, Helicopter Eela, and Lafangey Parindey.
- Sarkar received several accolades for his work, including the Filmfare Award for Best Art Direction and Zee Cine Award for Most Promising Director for Parineeta in 2005 and the Indira Gandhi Award for Best Debut Film of a Director in 2006.

Intel cofounder Gordon Moore passes away at 94

- Gordon Moore, who helped start the company Intel in 1968 and predicted that computing power would continue to increase over time (known as "Moore's Law"), has passed away at the age of 94.

- Moore was an important figure in the semiconductor industry and played a key role in putting Intel's processors in most personal computers.

Malayalam's comedy king Innocent passes away at 75

- A Malayalam comedy superstar Innocent Vareed Thekkethala, who acted in more than 750 films and served as an independent MP for the Chalakkudy constituency in the 16th Lok Sabha elections, has passed away at the age of 75.
- He was also the President of the Association of Malayalam Movie Artists (AMMA) for 18 years.
- His last film appearance was in the 2022 movie "Kaduva" with Prithviraj, and his final movie, "Paachuvum Albhuthavilakkum," is set to release on April 28.
- The actor was also a writer and published five books based on his life experiences. Innocent was a significant figure in the film industry, and he defeated Congress heavyweight PC Chacko in the 16th Lok Sabha elections but lost in 2019.

Miscellaneous News

10 yrs post-retirement, a life-size statue of Sachin Tendulkar at Wankhede

- A decade after his retirement, there is news about plans to install a life-size statue of Sachin Tendulkar inside the iconic Wankhede stadium where he played his last game for India.
- The statue will be unveiled on April 23. It will be the legend's 50th birthday.
- There is speculation that if everything does not work out well, the inauguration of the statue may be delayed until the 50-over World Cup planned later this year.

Two Australian Universities to set up Campuses in Gujarat's GIFT City

- Union Education Minister Dharmendra Pradhan announced that two Australian universities Wollongong and Deakin are set to establish campuses in Gujarat's 'GIFT City'.
- The two universities will sign an agreement on setting up their campuses during Australian Prime Minister Anthony Albanese's maiden visit to India next week.

'World's first' bamboo crash barrier installed on Maharashtra highway

- The world's first 200-metre-long bamboo crash barrier has been installed on a highway connecting Chandrapur and Yavatmal districts in Maharashtra.

- Named 'Bahu Balli', the bamboo crash barrier underwent "rigorous testing" at various government-run institutions like the National Automotive Test Tracks (NATRAX) in Pithampur, Indore.
- This was rated as Class 1 during the Fire Rating Test conducted at the Central Building Research Institute (CBRI) in Roorkee and it has also been accredited by the Indian Road Congress, According to Nitin Gadkari-led Ministry of Road Transport and Highways.

BSE and UN Women India launch FinEMPOWER programme

- FinEMPOWER, a new initiative from BSE and UN Women India, was introduced at the Bombay Stock Exchange (BSE).
- In order to empower women towards financial security, BSE and UN Women have collaborated on a year-long capacity-building programme.
- To increase investment in female leaders and entrepreneurs at BSE, BSE and UN Women India together organized the "Ring the Bell for Gender Equality ceremony" in observance of International Women's Day.

G20 flower festival begins in New Delhi

- Connaught Plaza in Delhi will host a Flower Festival beginning from, March 11. It aims to emphasise the diversity of G20 participants and invited nations.
- The festival, which is being held at Central Park and is being organised by the New Delhi Municipal Council, was opened today by Union Environment Minister Bhupender Yadav.
- Japan, Singapore, and the Netherlands are among the G20 nations taking part. The objective of the festival is to showcase the vibrancy and colourful display of G20 members and guest countries.

GoI Unveils Rs 1,18,500 Crore Budget for Jammu And Kashmir

- Union Finance Minister Nirmala Sitharaman has unveiled Rs 1,18,500 crore budget for Jammu & Kashmir Union Territory for the next financial year.
- The total budget estimates for the fiscal are Rs. 1,18,500 crores, of which developmental expenditure is of the order of Rs. 41,491 crores.
- The capital component of the budget has increased substantially.

Sampanna Ramesh sets record as fastest Indian to swim across Palk Strait

- Sampanna Ramesh Shelar, a Bachelor of Physical Education student, has set a new record by becoming the fastest Indian in the under-21 category to swim across the Palk Strait, from Talaimannar in Sri Lanka to Dhanuskodi in Tamil Nadu.
- He completed the 29 km distance in just 5 hours and 30 minutes, beating the previous record of 8 hours and 26 minutes.
- Shelar started his swim at 6:00 am on Thursday and reached Dhanushkodi at 11:26 am.
- He is coached by Mr. Jitendra Khasnis and plans to complete solo swims across the English and Catalina Channels to achieve the Oceans Seven Challenge.

Google Doodle celebrates 77th birth anniversary of late Kitty O'Neil

- Google Doodle: Kitty O'Neil, a famous American stuntwoman and actress who was deaf from a young age, was commemorated by Google on her 77th birthday anniversary with a doodle featuring her in a yellow jumpsuit.
- She went on to become one of Hollywood's most famous stunt drivers.
- Google celebrated Kitty O'Neil's 77th birth anniversary with a doodle that depicted her in a yellow jumpsuit.
- Despite being deaf since childhood, she became a well-known stunt driver in Hollywood and held the women's absolute land speed record until 2019.

Urban Climate Film Festival

- The National Institute of Urban Affairs (NIUA) has partnered with the Ministry of Housing & Urban Affairs, the French Development Agency (AFD), and the European Union to organize the first-ever Urban Climate Film Festival as part of the CITIIS program under U20 engagement events.
- The festival will feature a carefully selected collection of 11 films from 9 countries to increase public awareness of the effects of climate change on urban life and encourage discussion on sustainable urban development.
- On the 24th of March 2023, the M.L. Bhartia Auditorium at Alliance Française in Lodhi Estate, New Delhi, will host the inauguration of the Urban Climate Film Festival.

EC chooses transgender folk artiste Manjamma Jogati as poll icon for the community

- The Election Commission (EC) in the Indian state of Karnataka has selected Manjamma Jogati, a transgender folk dancer, as a poll icon to encourage more members of the transgender community to register and vote.
- Alongside Jogati, several other individuals, including cricketer Rahul Dravid and Jnanapeeth awardee Chandrashekar Kambar, have also been chosen as poll ambassadors.
- The number of registered transgender voters in Karnataka has increased significantly from 4,552 in 2018 to 42,756 in 2023.

'Ironman' Krishna Prakash becomes first person to swim from Gateway of India to Elephanta Caves

- As part of the 'Drowning Prevention Awareness' campaign, Indian Police Service (IPS) officer Krishna Prakash swam from Gateway of India to Elephanta Caves, Mumbai.
- He completed the expedition of 16.20 kms in just 5 hours 26 minutes and became the first person in history to do so.
- This is far from the first time the IPS officer broker broke records in sporting competitions. In 2017, he completed the Ironman Triathlon, one of the most challenging sports events in the world.
- This is a three-day event that requires the participants to complete a 3.8-kilometre swim, a 180.2-kilometer bicycle ride, and a 42.2 km run in 16–17 hours.
- This achievement earned Prakash the 'Iron Man' title and a mention in the World Book of Records.

Cheetah Sasha dies due to kidney ailment in MP's Kuno National Park

- A Namibian Cheetah passed away at Kuno National Park in MP, India.
- The cheetah, named Sasha, was reportedly in good health when it was moved to India on September 17th 2022, but it was discovered that it had a kidney infection.
- This event was a setback for the project aimed at rejuvenating the cheetah population in the country.

Indian-origin Sikh woman becomes Connecticut's first Asian assistant police chief

- Lt. Manmeet Colon, who is of Indian origin and a Sikh woman officer, has recently taken up the position of assistant police chief in the state of Connecticut, becoming the first-ever person of Asian descent to hold the position.
- She has been a member of the New Haven Police Department (NHPD) for 15 years and was appointed as the city's third assistant police chief in an official ceremony.

National Gallery of Modern Art to organise "Spring Fiesta" 2023 to celebrate 69 years of the Museum

- To commemorate the 69th anniversary of its official inauguration by Vice President Dr. S Radhakrishnan on March 29, 1954, the National Gallery of Modern Art in New Delhi will host its first-ever "Spring Fiesta" in 2023.
- The event will feature over 50 stalls set up on the museum lawns by individuals from various backgrounds who specialize in areas such as handicrafts, ceramics, indigenous art, fashion, and more.

Conservation Plan for Great Indian Bustards

- In order to conserve and protect the Great Indian Bustard, which is considered one of the largest flying birds in the world, the Government of India is implementing various measures throughout the country.
- However, apart from certain regions in Rajasthan and Gujarat, the bird has disappeared from 90% of its original habitat.
- The International Union for Conservation of Nature has classified the species as "critically endangered."

www.ingramcontent.com/pod-product-compliance
Ingram Content Group UK Ltd.
Pitfield, Milton Keynes, MK11 3LW, UK
UKHW061704190726
13853UKWH00008B/2401

9 789355 566492